The World of

the Virtuoso

MARC PINCHERLE

The World of
the Virtuoso

*Translated from the French
by Lucile H. Brockway*

W · W · NORTON & COMPANY · INC · *New York*

First Edition

This work was first published in French under the title
Le Monde des Virtuoses
Copyright © 1961 by Flammarion

Library of Congress Catalog Card No. 63-9882

Published simultaneously in the Dominion of
Canada by George J. McLeod Limited, Toronto.

PRINTED IN THE UNITED STATES OF AMERICA
FOR THE PUBLISHERS BY THE VAIL-BALLOU PRESS, INC.

1 2 3 4 5 6 7 8 9

TO
Andrea della Corte

Contents

Illustrations

Foreword

A LONG LIFE of concert going has made me more and more interested in the very diverse activities which take place in the concert hall, in the psychological, esthetic, and practical considerations which are put into play, in the physical phenomena which are present there, and which without doubt will be measurable in the near future. We shall then know how the density of the public, the configuration of the hall, the degree of heat, of dryness, or of humidity in the surrounding atmosphere act on the receptivity of the listener; by what sort of contagion the enthusiasm or coolness of a small group can unleash the enthusiasm of a crowd, or on the contrary, paralyze it.

I have long thought of undertaking a methodical research on this vast subject—the work of others, in particular my eminent colleague Andrea della Corte, has advanced very far. But the years pass, and I know that time will not allow me to realize this over-ambitious project. Here at least is some material consisting of studies either unpublished or published in various reviews, which I have brought up to date. It is addressed not to musicologists, but to all who love music and are interested in the artists who bring it to them. However it contains nothing which is not based on trustworthy documents.

The World of

the Virtuoso

I

Virtuosity

A CHARACTERISTIC trait of musical life today is the quasi-permanent quarrel that virtuosity provokes on the one hand between the large public which strongly favors it, and, on the other hand, the considerable number of writers, critics, and composers who like to see in it a sort of malady of growth, late come, engendered by Romanticism, and whose fatal consequence is the debasement of taste. Virtuosos and musicians confront each other like brothers who are enemies, each triumph of the one being repaid by a new humiliation from the other.

To verify or refute such allegations is not an easy thing on the pure esthetic level, unless we take up the old debate on the true nature of music: is it a sensual joy on the same order as gastronomy, or in essence "a veiled art, born of a dream, a reminiscence of the great unconscious universe?" It would be better perhaps to consider the facts.

A first surprise awaits us. "Virtuoso" in current usage means a skillful performer, but one limited to the practice of his instrument. However, the word appears to have had a much wider meaning in its original use in French. One meets it, coming from the Italian, in the *Memoirs* of Mme. de Motteville, applied to the singer and harpist Leonora Baroni, and a

little later in Molière's *The Sicilian* (1668). But it is defined
for the first time in the *Dictionnaire de Musique* by Sébastien
de Brossard in 1703:

Virtu means, in Italian, not only that propensity of the soul
which renders us agreeable to God and makes us act according to
the rules of right reason; but also that superiority of talent, skill,
or ability which makes us excel, be it in the theory or be it in the
practice of the Fine Arts, beyond those who apply themselves as
much as we do. It is from this word that the Italians have formed
the adjectives *virtuoso* or *virtudioso*, to name or praise those to
whom Providence has granted this excellence or superiority. Thus,
to them, an excellent painter, a skillful architect, etc., is a *Virtuoso*,
but they more commonly and more especially give this beautiful
name to the best musicians, and among them, rather to those who
apply themselves to the *theory* or to the composition of music
than to those who excel in the other arts, so that in their language
to say simply that a man is a *Virtuoso* is almost always to say that
he is an excellent musician.

Francesco Galeazzi, an excellent theoretician who is too
little known, writes in the same vein at the very end of the
century, in 1791. After having traced the plan of technical
studies necessary to form a violinist, he adds, "we have now
made a good musician in the material sense, a faithful ex-
ecutor, and we cannot yet accord him the title of 'virtuoso'
which belongs only to those who possess the inventive genius
proper to the art."

Since that time the meaning of the word has strangely
narrowed. Under the name of virtuosity, one condemns the
total subservience of the work to the interpreter—"a physical
pleasure, a pleasure in skill, in agility, in satisfying muscular

activity, a pleasure in conquering, in dazzling, in subjugating by his person the thousand-headed public . . . a pleasure mortal to art and to the soul." (Romain Rolland, *Jean-Christophe*, IV, 41.)

A pleasure, in any case, not of recent invention, as it is fashionable to say, but almost as old as music itself: for virtuosity existed before the words that label it, just as snobbism did before Thackeray's immortal pamphlet.

One can presume that in all countries—and ethnography gives us many assurances—when the art of singing or playing some instrument had barely taken shape, a rivalry arose among the most gifted performers, and that certain of them excited an admiration which served as a stimulant and contributed in the highest degree to progress in their primitive technique.

It is difficult not to see in the legends of Amphion, Arion, and Orpheus a reflection of those ancient glories that were acquired by particularly inspired singers and players at a time when music and magic were still closely linked. But in the first historical epochs we are in possession of more positive facts. Six centuries before the Christian era certain Greek aulos players (players of a double oboe) were renowned and feted more than a Horowitz, an Oistrakh, a Callas. They went from city to city, royally paid, consenting to give lessons to a privileged few for a fee in gold, dazzling the crowd by the sometimes extravagant pomp of their clothes and jewels. And even then their programs tended toward descriptive music, which concert artists of the baser epochs have always exploited with profit.

In ancient Rome, foreign virtuosos created a sensation. The Emperor Vespasian, always miserly, gave 200,000 ses-

terces to two cithara players. Another cithara player, Mene-
crates, got from Nero a palace and a fortune. Mark Anthony
gave to Anaxenor, also a cithara player, the right to levy
tribute on four cities and to have at his disposal a guard of
soldiers. In the time of Augustus an Egyptian harpist, Ho-
roudja, had enough influence to foment a revolution in Thebes.

And even in these remote times there was the inevitable
professional degeneration, not only in the exaggerated sump-
tuousness of dress: a certain aulos player, a contemporary of
Aeschylus, made himself ridiculous by his refusal to give place
to the singers, another by his cunning in placing a claque in the
audience.

One could enumerate without end the half-historic, half-
legendary musicians of the high Middle Ages whom their
sovereigns pampered and arrayed in sumptuous garments, like
the harpists of the Irish king, Connaire Mor, who were dressed
in light blue and adorned with silver necklaces, with crystal
rings, and brooches and buckles of gold. Or those of Islam,
that singer from Medina named Djemilah, who, when she left
for Mecca, was escorted by a brilliant train of artists, notables,
and fifty slave musicians sent by the great ladies of the city;
and M'abed, the singer who received 12,000 pieces of gold
from a sultan the first time he heard him; and El Mauceli,
who earned millions with his lute and his voice; and Ishak, at
whose death the Caliph exclaimed: "Now that he is gone, the
Empire has lost an ornament and a glory!"

An instrumental virtuosity arose in the West as early as the
twelfth century, no longer solely on the part of the minstrels
who were obliged by their profession to play various instruments, nor even the troubadours, for whom the instrument

was the indispensable auxiliary of the poem they declaimed
or sang. And this instrumental virtuosity was already tending
in the direction in which we see it go farther and farther. Read
the praises which Giraldus Cambrensis bestowed on some Irish
harpists in 1183: "They are incomparably more skillful than
those of any other nation. Their manner is neither slow nor
harsh, but rapid and lively. . . . They astonish us by the way
they observe rhythm and accents with such quick movements.
They delight the listener with such delicacy and such sweetness that the supreme skill of their art seems to be to dis-
simulate it."

Here is a comment on Francesco Landino, a blind organist
of immense reputation in the fourteenth century: "He starts
to play with incomparable art and great sweetness, and although deprived of the light of his eyes, with such speed that
he surpasses all other organists whom one can remember."

Charm and speed: this formula has proved itself ever since.
And do not think that the virtuoso is ignorant of the relation
between the exploitation of this recipe and the success it as-
sures him.

There is too great a tendency to see in the search for effect,
for success, a modern weakness. Prior to the eighteenth century, we are sometimes told, public concerts hardly existed,
and performers were spared in some measure the temptation
to shine. What of the church, especially in Italy, where the
organist, who sometimes played the harpsichord too, the violinist or the viol player (Maugars, for example) played before thousands of the faithful, not all of them absorbed by the
thought of their salvation to the point of forgetting to listen?
And what of the princely courts where violent rivalries were

established as to who had the best lute player or the best harpsichordist, an Albert de Rippe or a Chambonnières, heaped with honors and gifts?

Indeed the church was, albeit paradoxically, the chosen field of virtuosity. Are not the calls to order that one finds in such numbers in the parish archives testimony to the skill of performers who were too brilliant?

The church toccatas are one of the products of this tendency toward virtuosity, disciplined among the masters by good taste and respect for holy ground. But this did not mean that the musicians were unmindful of the impression they produced. The great Frescobaldi, publishing his *Toccate*, addresses to the performer certain recommendations, some of which treat of the purity of expression, while others, such as this, clearly focus on success: "Before playing a run in sixteenth notes for two hands, stop for a moment on the preceding note, even if it is short. Then resolutely play the run, thus showing to best advantage the agility of your hands."

The Olympian Bach played very fast, as we know. Perhaps he took no pleasure in dazzling his contemporaries and was content to prove only to himself the beauty of his light, precise, and well-regulated technique, a mode of execution one would call sportive, if that were not an anachronism. But was it not for sport that he lent himself, in the manner of the times, to two musical duels, against Heitmann at Hamburg, and against Kauffmann and Schott at Leipzig, to say nothing of the near encounter with Marchand?

Others, more human, did not hide their desire to display their technique, and to please the greatest number. In publishing his pieces for the harpsichord, Daquin announced that there were among them "those which are for playing in the grand manner"; the one entitled *The Three Cadences* is, he says, "of a taste which I can assure you is new, extraordinary, and has never before appeared in music." In Rameau, the title alone, *The Three Hands*, shows evidence of his intention to produce an artifice of virtuosity (a crossing of hands in imitation of the Italians) which heightens the interest for the listener-spectator.

Well before the Romantic era, then, virtuosity was aware of itself; it sought to please. The musician shut in his ivory tower who created without thought of his effect on the public was not in the current style. François Couperin the Great offers us a confession many masters could countersign, when, in *l'Art de toucher le clavecin*, (*The Art of Playing the Harpsichord*), he compares music written for ensemble playing with pieces written for a soloist: "If it were a question of choosing between the accompaniment and the solo pieces, to bring one or the other to perfection, I feel that *amour-propre* would make me prefer the solo pieces to the accompaniment. I agree that nothing is more amusing for oneself and binds us more to others than to be a good accompanist. But what an injustice! He is the last one hired for a concert . . . while someone who excels in the solo pieces enjoys all to himself the attention and the applause."

Evidently the slope is perilous. Not for a François Couperin; first, he is his own interpreter, and he is spared the danger of seeing his thought deformed by any other performer. Further, in that part of their work where they deliberately make sacrifices to virtuosity, Haydn, Mozart, Weber, Chopin, et al., will have their genius as a safeguard.

But there are others, who multiply from the middle of the eighteenth century at an accelerated rate. Up till then, the role of the interpreter hardly existed apart from that of the composer. Each virtuoso wrote for himself, except in the rare cases where the prestige of a greater name could guarantee him a more marked success, as when Carbonelli and Geminiani made themselves champions of Corelli, or Guignon played Vivaldi; or Pagin, Tartini. At the very least, no one set himself up as an interpreter who did not have a thorough knowledge of theory and composition, which, to tell the truth, were less complex and difficult to assimilate than in our day. To make a place as a harpsichordist or an organist, one had to be able to realize a figured bass and to ornament the melody at sight. The palest shadows of Frescobaldi, of Bach, of Couperin were complete musicians.

Around 1730–1760, musical life was completely transformed; public concerts multiplied; virtuosos began making concert tours; the audience became larger (in such a situation, the display of culture goes in inverse ratio to its depth: present-day television quiz shows furnish us with a good example); music publishing spread; Leipzig, Paris, Vienna, and London surpassed in activity the first centers of Italy and Holland.

The enormous multiplication of virtuosos which resulted from this new state of things could not be paralleled by an equal flowering of composers. The non-composing virtuosos did not capitulate for all that; they made up elaborate pieces of little value in which they limited themselves to making their instrument shine. "The only disappointment that one experienced at the Concert Spirituel in the past fortnight [Easter,

1782]," writes an anonymous critic in the *Almanach musical,* "comes from the license with which beginning artists are allowed to play Symphonies and Concertos of their own composition which present only puerile images in childish frames, reminiscences of pieces already heard, cut, pieced, and sewn to other reminiscences. . . ."

The natural result was, in the nineteenth century, the enormous literature of Fantasies, Potpourris, *Souvenirs of Norma,* of *La Sonnambula,* etc., which comprise the basis of the concerts of Herz, Kalkbrenner, Steibelt, but also of Liszt: a Beethoven sonata is to be found in his programs only when surrounded by futilities of that order. I have before me the program of the Sunday matinee of May 3, 1835, when Liszt came to enhance by his presence the concert Berlioz gave to reintroduce his *Symphonie fantastique.* Liszt played only once, as an interlude. One of his own concertos? a Beethoven concerto? No, a *Solo di Bravura* on *Alexander's March* by Moscheles!

This was the period when the greatest pianist of Europe, Marie Pleyel, could put on her programs the *Regata* by Rossini, the *Rataplan* and the *Blessing of the Daggers* from *Les Huguenots,* in which descriptive music triumphs, *A Naval Battle, The Battle of Prague, The Battle of Nerwinde,* with trumpet calls, cannonades (expressed by hitting the basses indistinctly with the flat of both hands), cries of the wounded and dying, fanfares of victory, etc. A set of drums, triangle, and cymbals was affixed to the piano and controlled by means of extra pedals.

But again, all this was not an innovation of the nineteenth century, nor of Romanticism, to which we can no longer attribute the attitudes of virtuosos, their publicity-seeking extravagances: the eighteenth century had had worse.

Only the gesticulations of some of our orchestra conductors can be compared with those of the Italian virtuosos as described by Rameau's nephew, or with those of Locatelli, who, according to a contemporary letter, played with such furious energy that he had to use several dozen violins a year. . . .

As for ostentatious dress, whom could we find to equal the violinist Abraham Fisher, as described by Lady Morgan in her memoirs?

"A foreign servant preceded him, dressed in brilliant livery, carrying a violin case of red and gold leather. The celebrated virtuoso followed, walking on the tips of his toes. He wore a brown silk tunic bound in scarlet and decorated with sparkling buttons. His hair was powdered and perfumed, and dressed so high that his small face seemed cut in two. His breeches were fastened at the knee with diamond buttons. His presence saturated the air with perfumes. . . ."

The amiable Victor Gilles continued the tradition of these same singularities, which seem very discreet when we remember those of Lolli, of Scheller, of Michel Esser, of Jarnovick, which filled volumes of collected table-talk!

As to the essential, by which I mean the musical content of the concerts, frivolity can no longer be charged solely against the 1830s. In the vocal polyphony of the Renaissance, side by side with the great descriptive masterpieces of Janequin (whose technical perfection perhaps hides some concessions to entertainment pure and simple), what inconsequential knickknacks, openly designed to amuse!

In the eighteenth century this disposition grew, at least

among those wandering virtuosos who went from city to city and had to catch the curiosity of the public at first sight. The father of the young Mozart was seeking just that when he announced at Frankfurt, on August 30, 1763, that his seven-year-old son, after playing the harpsichord and the violin, accompanied by "symphonies," would play on a harpsichord whose keyboard was covered with a cloth, just as if he had the keys before his eyes, would guess notes and chords from a distance, and would improvise as long as one wanted. Jacob Scheller promised to imitate on the violin the sound of a harmonica and a fishwives' quarrel. Michel Esser triumphed in an imitation of the psaltery and the evocation of the fairy Urgèle, at sixty, eighty, and one hundred years. Lolli, when age had diminished the brilliance of his talent, made up for it by imitating, in the finale of his concerts, sometimes a parrot, sometimes a dog, sometimes a cat. His *Cat's Concerto* was such a success that managers of theaters in Vienna had to forbid the musicians to play the famous *glissando* like a cat's miaow that Lolli had made all the rage.

I call as next witness Karl Stamitz, son of the famous Johann Stamitz, and like his father a figure in the development of the pre-Classical symphony and a composer of some importance. Here, reproduced in its entirety, is the announcement of a concert he gave on the 29th of October, 1785, in Hamburg, the birthplace of German opera, the city where Handel, Mattheson, Telemann, and so many others became famous:

A grand musical entertainment, of which the first part, as in ordinary concerts, will be executed in a serious manner. But the second part, since the honored public likes also to be amused by comic subjects, will be played by Maestro Stamitz in a pantomime style, entirely new and untried.

FIRST PART

1. A new and majestic symphony, after which Mademoiselle Brandès will be heard.
2. Mr. Stamitz will play a solo on the viola and the viola d'amore. Because of public demand he will also play the *Marlborough*.

SECOND PART

A pantomime in a forest setting, with statues of Apollo and the Graces, with a medley of serious and comic variations. In the middle of the pantomime Mr. Stamitz will play, on all the instruments in turn, divers airs with variations, such as the well-loved *romance* from *Figaro*.

And if my reader is not yet sufficiently enlightened as to the fantasy which reigned in the concerts of a period when Classicism produced its greatest masterpieces and when musical Romanticism was already in the wings, let him glance at the announcement of a gala concert given in Vienna at the Theater "An der Wien" on December 23, 1806. It will be seen that this concert, organized for the benefit of Franz Clement, musical director of that theater and moreover a violin virtuoso of European reputation, was the concert at which the world first heard the Concerto in D major, Opus 61, by Beethoven, which appeared on the program between an unpublished overture by Méhul and an air by Mozart. The first part of the program was completed by fragments from Handel's *Ode for Saint Cecilia's Day*, orchestrated by Mozart—a choice, then, of the purest taste.

But in the second half, in addition to an overture and a vocal quartet by Cherubini, and another fragment from the *Ode for Saint Cecilia's Day*, it was announced that "Mr. Clement will improvise on the violin, and will play a sonata on a single string, holding the instrument upside down. . . ."

It is understandable that in all times the exaggerations and divagations of virtuosity have made it susceptible to violent hatreds, most variously and unequally founded.

Among the anti-virtuosos of antiquity, the Latin writers Cicero, Livy, Suetonius, and naturally the satirists Horace, Juvenal, and Martial railed against the excessive rewards given to foreign entertainers.

Saint Augustine was perhaps more violent. He vilified the aulos players and invoked against them the elementary musical sense of the public at large. "Do you believe," he writes, "that the aulos player is gifted with as much sense? His trained fingers obey his memory; he plays only as well as are dominant in him the faculties which reason tells us are dominant in the beasts: memory, instinct, and the ability to imitate."

Such severity is explained by the disproportion which existed between the quality of the art of these popular virtuosos and the adulation they aroused, an adulation blind, without nuances, and no less revolting than that awarded today to movie stars, boxers, and accordion players, who are taken up by the masses as brusquely as they will be rejected and forgotten. Moreover, Saint Augustine wrote his treatise *On Music* at the very time of his conversion. It is normal that the ardor of the neophyte should turn against the amusements which as a profane youth he had had the weakness to admit or to love.

In the Middle Ages there developed another sort of antagonism, that which opposed the creator to the interpreter, the composer to the singer. "Between them," writes Guido d'Arezzo, "the distance is great, one doing nothing but express, the other knowing what it is to compose. He who does what he cannot understand can be called an animal. . . ."

This rancor runs through all the ages. In all times the creator, who has worked in solitude, ignored by the public and in a sense sacrificed, will have reason to envy those who present themselves to the crowd and gather to themselves its applause and remuneration.

Although he was a virtuoso by profession, Geminiani, in his *Rules for Playing in a True Taste*, complains that in England "the hand is more highly regarded than the brain, the interpreter than the composer." In Italy this attitude was almost universal. The *Teatro alla moda* by Marcello makes it stand out in clear-cut terms, and Quantz very objectively states that "French music depends more on the composition than on the execution; Italian music depends almost as much on the execution as on the composition, and in some pieces more so." This latitude awarded to the interpreter naturally entailed a correspondingly greater favor.

In this respect, the separation of the two functions, composition and execution, solved nothing; quite the contrary. When Richard Wagner arrived in Paris, full of ideas, with numerous works in his portfolio, and poor as Job, he ran up against the full triumph of the champions of execution, not only Liszt, Chopin, and Paganini, but the Kalkbrenners and the Herzes. He expressed his bitterness in a long article, *On Virtuosos*, in which he says this: "The obligation imposed on composers to arrange their works in the interest of such and such a special quality of the interpreter is sad enough. But the situation is far worse. The musician who wants to gain the sympathy of the crowds is forced to keep uppermost in his mind that intractable self-love which is characteristic of all virtuosos, and to reconcile the miracles that are expected of his genius with such a servitude."

Let us skip a good half-century, to a time just after 1900. In every country, good taste in music, although not so widespread as in literature or in the plastic arts, has made notable progress. The virtuosos' repertory has been purged of the monstrosities of the period of 1840.

Soloists are held in no less favor, but they have become more dignified. A minority clings to the sterile acrobatics of the histrionic technique. The others take as their models Ysaÿe, Risler, Paderewski, Pugno, men who are accomplished musicians, who awaken talents, launch new works, and to whom the evolution of our art owes a great deal.

It is at this moment that there arose a violent crisis of anti-virtuosity, in what was called the "War of the Concertos." There was, as there still is in symphonic programs, an abuse of concertos, less in the sense of the intrusion of bad concertos than in the too frequent use of good ones. Against that abuse certain objectors began to agitate in 1902 in the lobby of the Concerts Lamoureux, then elsewhere, until one day at the Concerts Colonne, on March 24, 1904, they brought the thunder of the law upon themselves when they hissed Paderewski in the Beethoven Concerto in G. Their trial raised an inquiry, on the part of their lawyer, Maître Bonzon, whose results were not what they had counted on. The demonstrators accused the concerto of being an inferior kind of music, corrupted by virtuosity. Only d'Indy gave them his approval, while condemning (softly) the form of their manifestations. Saint-Saëns took a stand for the concerto and for virtuosity. But the strongest response was that of Fauré, who because of his human and artistic personality was so reserved and so little prone to put himself forward, and the less inclined to defend the concerto, one would have thought, since he himself had never published one.

However, he defended it firmly, ending with this point: "I should not like to forget those compositions of César Franck and Vincent d'Indy which, though they do not carry the title of concerto, require the use of a solo instrument with the orchestra, demanding on the part of the player an absolute virtuosity."

An indiscriminate mistrust of virtuosity is not dead. In 1935 at the Châtelet, I heard again the war cry "Down with the concerto!" between two movements of Beethoven's Violin Concerto. But between times, anti-virtuosity has acquired a literary elegance. In his *Pensées sur la Musique*, André Suarès executed a series of brilliant variations on this theme: "How impure is the virtuoso! How stupid he is! And the more he pushes himself forward, the more useless he seems. Among virtuosos, the most vain is the one who least desires to be vain; he tries to efface himself before the work; he is the only one who does not see that he acts as a screen; he undoubtedly believes that he is transparent. His modesty is all that is most immodest. He dare not choose between the work and himself.

However, the very fact of being a virtuoso implies a choice: a soloist interprets only according to his own nature . . . ," and more of the same, up to a certain passage where Suarès rails against "the violinist-boxer who plays the adagio of a Bach concerto swooning on his double-stops."

Double-stops? But no adagio in the violin concertos of Bach requires double-stops. The double-stops are there only for the cadence of the phrase, a simple burst of verbal virtuosity, which takes away from Suarès's diatribe much of the importance it might have had. Many anti-virtuosos are of the same stripe, following vague preconceived ideas, among which it would be tempting to try to impose some order.

In condemning virtuosity lock, stock, and barrel, without appeal or nuances, it seems as if one were obeying mainly the tyrannical mania to draw up a hierarchy. On the top level one puts the musical idea, the "pure" idea, separated from its material, "a reflection of the great unconscious universe," and far below it, the realization of that idea—the instrument, the instrumentalist, technical skill, virtuosity.

This is to forget what music in its beginnings may have owed to improvisation, which doubtless long preceded not only all conscious and systematic art, but also the first sketchy writing. What might not have been, then, the importance of virtuosity! He who says "improvisation" declares at the same time the ascendancy of manual dexterity, the constant straining toward new prowess, up to the moment when a particularly happy song, a particularly welcome and widely admired passage can be adopted as a model.

Periodically, it happens that the temptation to virtuosity

passes the limit, that the less gifted are maladroit in imitating the masters, and there follows a decline, from which there is a reaction, a counter-offensive in the direction of purity. Let us observe in passing that this process takes place in many other fields, including composition. It was the abuse of contrapuntal virtuosity (Masses in forty-eight parts with twelve choirs and other such monstrosities) which at the end of the Renaissance provoked a brutal revolt against polyphonic writing and brought on the writing of accompanied melody. Another example closer to us is the proliferation of the orchestra in Strauss, Mahler, and Bruckner which oriented Schoenberg toward the small orchestra of soloists.

In poetry, in the theater, in the plastic arts, the same causes have engendered similar effects.

To return to reactions more specifically musical, we need only go back to the time of the Renaissance when the first autonomous instrumental style of which we have any knowledge began to be elaborated. We know how the first instrumental virtuosos were inspired by vocal polyphony, transcribing sacred and secular songs and adapting them according to the resources of their instrument and their own ingenuity.

How many times at this critical moment did technique precede inspiration, the hand advance before the brain! The organist may have desired nothing more than to realize the equivalent of the vocal quartet. But he had a keyboard under his fingers. The range of the voice no longer counted for him: the equality and facility gained from this keyboard incited him to wide displacements of the hands; new harmonic progressions resulted, born as much by chance as from his own conscious will: and behold, the first free forms—the preludes, canzoni, toccatas of Claudio Merulo, Diruta, and others, in which one can perceive amid vestiges of the contrapuntal discipline, the soaring of a new activity, a playful activity which the rules will later restrict. And this holds true for the classical forms, the sonata and the concerto, at the beginning simple diversions of virtuosos, which with the passage of time become more ordered, more complicated, enriched to the point of hypertrophy by a skill which in the second stage of its evolution often reverts to a dried-up formula.

At the first stage of virtuosity, the influence of the hand is sovereign. Old Father Mersenne saw it clearly when he wrote, in the second book of his *Traité des instruments:* "The art or the science and industry of the hand is so great that several have called it one of the principal instruments of wisdom and of reason," and he obligingly reproduced this passage from a treatise on the lute by his friend, Basset: "The skillful hands of lutenists remind me of the opinion of Anaxagoras, who thought human wisdom was embodied in the hands. But men are not wise because they have hands; rather they have them in order to be wise, in order to execute what art and reason dictate."

How many composers can flatter themselves that they have not benefited from this shaping of thought by matter, this aid that the fingers can give to the musical idea, if only through those delightful harmonic progressions vainly sought in the abstract, pen in hand, that a favorable chance let them pick from the keyboard in a moment of careless reverie?

There are many other aspects of this same question to examine. One of the most curious is the force with which instruments stamp with their mark not only works destined for them, but, at certain privileged periods of their evolution, the repertory of other instruments. The German violinists of the seventeenth century wrote for a long time in the style of the organ (while J. S. Bach, the organist, often harked back to the violin); the French harpsichordists, up to Chambonnières and even beyond, were influenced by the style of the lute, and reproduced for that reason, although their instrument did not demand it, its hesitations, syncopations, and open harmonies. Later, with the invasion of the Italian sonata, they imitated the figurations of the violin, arpeggios and other broken-chord figures, to the point where François Couperin had to remind them of the particular properties of bowed instruments. And when the success of the harpsichord was at its peak in France, around 1750, the organ tried to rival it in lightness and brilliance.

Over and above the details of instrumental writing, certain rules of composition reflect similar origins—the tonal unity of the dance suites of the sixteenth century certainly originated in the difficulty of changing the tuning of the instruments in the course of playing them.

The development of technique for technique's sake is also responsible for improvements in instrument-making, which steadily seeks increased sonority, suppleness, volubility, and color. As Anton Rubinstein remarks, "When Beethoven in his Sonata Opus 110, at the beginning of the adagio, indicates that one should strike a certain note twenty-eight times, it is a notice given by the virtuoso to the makers of pianos that they must discover a means of prolonging the sound on this instrument." Of notices of this kind, Bach, Scarlatti, Mozart, Chopin, and Liszt were prodigal.

And here virtuosity is a close neighbor of expressive power. A writer on esthetics, Lionel Landry, has said: "The decorative [for which we substitute "music of pure charm"] is often formed from the threadbare expressive, just as the living language is formed on the dead bodies of poetic metaphors." This is true. But the inverse is not less true. How simple figurations invented for their acrobatic appeal can become vehicles of expression can be studied in almost every measure of the works for unaccompanied violin by J. S. Bach; he borrows from J. J. Walther, from Biber, from the Italians—arpeggios, ornaments, double-stops, of little musical significance where he finds them: and he breathes music into them. The most characteristic example is the "bariolage" toward the end of the great Chaconne: it is an artifice which consists in sustaining unchanged during a whole phrase or a whole development a tone on an open string which acts as a pedal point. The others hardly use it except to demonstrate the suppleness of their bowing. With Bach, it produces a dynamic gradation and at the same time a sort of emotional crescendo of the rarest quality.

In modern instrumental literature one can find a thousand similar examples. It will suffice to point out the difference, from the point of view of expression, between Liszt's *Fountains of the Villa d'Este*, and the poor results his rivals obtained from experiments oriented in the same direction, and to wonder if Ravel, without the precedent of Liszt, would have had at his disposal so subtle a palette for his own *Fountains*.

But some good minds accord virtuosity a much more important creative role. In his *Esquisse d'un éloge de la Virtuosité*

(*Sketch for a Eulogy on Virtuosity*, a speech delivered at Nice on May 27, 1940, in commemoration of the death of Paganini), Paul Valéry declared:

"One forgets too often that art exists only in the act; art is action; it is this action whose goal is to excite and modify the sensibilities of man and to obtain those developments that make themselves indefinitely desired. . . . To say that art is action is to say indirectly that a work of art is in itself only a formula for action. In this state, the most beautiful work is only what it is—whether one sees in it only signs on paper; whether, knowing how to read those signs, one can not or does not wish to communicate to this reading what it needs in actual and appropriate human energy to produce on the sensibilities those effects of resonance which I indicated in three words a moment ago. This work which is still only writing has therefore only a potential existence. It is a check drawn on the store of talent of an eventual artist. It is also comparable to a mechanism that is reduced to a system of arbitrarily assembled solid bodies, if one refrains from applying to it the forces which the inventor had planned. . . . Texts or scores are only, in effect, systems of conventional signs, each syllable or note of which should instigate the act to which it corresponds. The quality of each of these acts, that of their inner connection and their mysterious interdependence, depends entirely on the person who acts, and who achieves the transmutation of the potential work into the real work.

"I shall make on this point a remark I think rather interesting: that there is no great work which is not susceptible to a large variety of equally plausible interpretations. The richness of the work lies in the number of meanings or values it can receive while remaining itself. Thus the virtuoso is the one who, par excellence, gives life and reality to what was only writing, available to any comer, to the ignorance, the clumsiness, the insufficient comprehension of any comer. The virtuoso renders the work incarnate . . ."

This is undoubtedly going rather far. For a musician, the reading of a score translates itself into a "mental audition," that can attain the presence of a live performance.

Furthermore, progress in mechanical music, and especially in electronic music, allows us to foresee the time when the composer can fix, down to the last detail, the interpretation "ne varietur" of his music. In 1928 (*Comoedia*, February 25), Honegger invoked collaboration with the machine in these words:

"I firmly believe that musicians will be obliged to have more and more recourse to mechanical diffusion . . . In our times, the listener no longer goes to hear a Beethoven symphony, but to hear Mr. X . . . in that symphony. The score no longer has any importance. Symphonic concerts, as Gabriel Pierné has said, live more and more on soloists. People come to applaud the tight-rope dancer. The dancer is everything; the immortal work is only the rope which serves for his exercises, sometimes his fantasies.

"Suppose that Beethoven, using modern inventions, could himself record on a perforated tape his own work and his own interpretation. Would it not be very moving for us to hear it? Do you not find it odious that a creative musician should be obliged to pass through the filter of another musician who plays his work? In painting would a picture-framer permit himself to retouch the colors of a painting?

"Mechanical music permits the establishment of the master-interpretation. The future is with the completely mechanical orchestra, which will offer first the advantage of being no longer limited by the human possibilities of extent and duration. . . . I believe in the future of the mechanical in the domain of music, in the development of machine-made music, and perhaps—perhaps —in the resurrection of the lyric theater by modern scientific methods, which alone are capable of solving the problems created by the growing demands of human interpreters."

"By suppressing them?"

"Yes."

We are not there yet. We still have a need for virtuosity, whose appeal is not limited to the solo performance. We would hear neither the *Nocturnes* of Debussy, nor *Petrushka*, nor *Daphnis*, still less many scores of the various contemporary schools, if the hundred musicians of the orchestra had not frayed their fingers on the passage work of concertos, in the hope (frustrated nine times out of ten) of performing these same concertos as virtuoso soloists before the great public.

Here, then, are some of the merits of virtuosity in the present state of things. The most important without doubt is its role in the diffusion of music. And here, I confess, I understand Suarès not at all. For, after all, the number of people capable of reading music and drawing pleasure from the reading alone is infinitesimal. On whom then does he count to hear it performed? On amateurs? By definition, they do not perform in public, and are no help to us. And would the best of them exist without the stimulation of professional virtuosos?

These virtuosos count for a great deal in forming and building up audiences, on which, in the last analysis, the material life of music depends: without this public, even music publishing would wither and die. Then, O virtuosos of the pen, O Suarès, how would you know that masterpieces exist?

Given the way in which the instruction and the musical

culture of the public are assured—or more exactly, are not
assured—it would be vain to hope for audiences composed entirely of initiates. The virtuoso soloist is more accessible because he is less abstract, and so can lead beginners, by an out-
ward charm that is more effective than any constraint, to perfect their musical culture and to set themselves ever higher
goals.

It remains to speak of the specific eloquence of the true
virtuoso, of his force of persuasion, of the authority he radiates
even before he begins to play. Fétis, a hundred years ago,
wrote on this point with singular power: "I do not know what
emotion spreads through the atmosphere to announce the
presence of genius, but one is rarely mistaken. I am sure that I
will be understood by many of my readers."

The recent notion of invisible waves, of multiple systems
which surround us and bind us to others of like minds, today
makes this conception quite plausible. A long time ago now,
Emile Vuillermoz proposed in the case of Lauri-Volpi the
hypothesis of a magnetic fluid independent of his vocal art,
strictly speaking, and insisted that science would one day define it: a Paderewski, a Cortot, a Kreisler, a Casals, a Segovia
had it or have it still. Now, the most beneficial influence of this
fluid, or whatever one wants to call it, is to prepare the terrain
in which music can fix itself and germinate. Creating an immediate sympathy, it binds the isolated members of the audience into a homogeneous and unified whole, in which those
elements most refractory to musical emotion become amenable
to it, if only for a short moment.

Such is the major benefit of virtuosity, and one which
should bring it a greater regard than it gets from its critics.

It seems that they confuse it at their pleasure with its exaggerated form, which has been called *virtuosoism*. But even this virtuosoism has not all the faults imputed to it. It is not a sickness; it is only a symptom. It appears when music itself is sick, when taste is no longer a guide.

The display of virtuosity is perhaps a response on the part of the virtuoso and the composer to the demands of a frivolous public, which wants to be amused. Let us not proceed to impute to it the impoverishment of music: it should be considered under the same heading as the abuse of Franck's modulations by his followers, or the garlands of ninths in the hands of Debussy's imitators.

The defects of virtuosity correspond to some weakness in human nature, the desire to shine, to dazzle at small cost, which is to be found also in bad writers, bad lawyers, bad politicians, bad composers. The development of these defects corresponds to certain periods in the evolution of civilization. It would be unfair to condemn something which taken all in all is fruitful, for the abuses to which it, like everything else, is exposed.

Virtuosity, at the dawn of modern instrumental art, was one of the great mainsprings of music. We owe to it the creation of important forms and a never-ceasing competition which generates progress. Even its lowest incarnations have brought new resources to our true creative geniuses. And in conclusion, I beg pardon for having arrived at what seems to me a truism: there can be virtuosity without music, there can not be, there could not have been, music without virtuosity. The whole thing is to choose as perfect examples not Lolli, Steibelt, or Kalkbrenner, but Frescobaldi, Bach, Mozart, François Couperin.

II

Concerts

NOTHING is simpler, at first sight, than the notion of a concert; nothing more fleeting, when one tries to be precise. Littré's definition: "Concert: a gathering where a certain number of vocal or instrumental pieces are performed" seems unnecessarily cautious; but those proposed by the musical dictionaries are either vague (*Grove's Dictionary of Music:* "Musical performance more or less public") or err on the side of inaccuracy (*Harvard Dictionary of Music:* "Public performance of music meant for a large audience")— which would exclude those intimate gatherings in the time of the Renaissance of four, five, or six musicians seated around a table, with the parts of some song by Janequin or Lassus in front of them. They sang or plucked the lute for a little circle of connoisseurs, but just as often for their own pleasure, without an audience of any kind.

A famous engraving by Abraham Bosse marvelously evokes these intimate concerts, and one can find other representations by the hundreds from the fifteenth through the eighteenth centuries.

"Public performance given by one or more musicians at a place other than the church or the theater" (*Dictionnaire de Musique*, by Michel Brenet) does not satisfy us either. We can

41

overlook "at a place other than the theater," although in the eighteenth century one often heard concertos for violin, viola d'amore, or oboe during the entr'actes of operas. But "at a place other than the church"? Yes, if one considers it certain that strictly liturgical songs have no other object nor any other effect than to establish a dialogue between the believer and his God; on the other hand, as soon as musical developments intervene, when monophony is extended by ornamental melismas, when polyphony appears, and with even greater reason, when instruments come on the scene, it is difficult to believe that an esthetic emotion does not superimpose itself on the religious sentiment, and even efface it for a time.

In the seventeenth century Frescobaldi's organ attracted tens of thousands of listeners to St. Peter's in Rome; a little later the sonata and the concerto penetrated the church with their virtuosity and all that that implies of the appeal to success, of rivalry in technique, of wounds to vanity, of quarrels over precedence. Then the holy place was well and truly transformed into a concert hall; and one wonders how many of the faithful could have been in a contemplative mood that day in 1801, in the church of San Martino in Lucca, when the young Paganini, immediately after the Kyrie, launched into a concerto twenty-eight minutes long, in the course of which, according to the priest who reported the event, "he imitated on his violin the songs of birds, the sound of flutes, trumpets, and horns, so well that the concert became a sort of comic opera."

Neither the size of the hall nor the number of performers furnishes us with additional criteria. A recital by Andrés Segovia is a concert fully as much as those monster manifestations organized in Boston in 1869 and in 1872 by Patrick

Gilmore, when that daring bandmaster, outdoing Berlioz's most far-fetched dreams, grouped 10,000 voices and 1,000 instruments for the first concert, and for the second, 20,000 voices and 2,000 instruments. . . . So the wisest course is to fall back on Littré's definition, which does not define much, but which at any rate does not exclude anything, and to try to see under what aspects the concert has presented itself in the course of the centuries.

There is every chance that it was born with the first babblings of civilization, and that the first men who drew simple tunes and rhythms from their voices, from a slit reed, the trunk of a hollowed tree, or a taut string, attracted a group of listeners neither more nor less eccentric than those at our sessions of avant-garde music today.

What we shall never know is the psychological effect of these concerts and the uses to which they were put. At a slightly more advanced stage they are to be found associated with magic, with religious ceremonials, with processions of warriors, or communal rejoicings.

Among the Sumero-Chaldeans, from the fourth millennium on, we know of the existence of sacred concerts, with choirs and solo singers, of other concerts that enlivened banquets, of others that accompanied military reviews, and had a definite religious significance. Among the many bas-reliefs on the subject of music there is one from Kuyundshik (seventh century B.C.), now in the British Museum, which shows the triumph of an Assyrian general placed by his sovereign on the throne of the king of Susa, whom he has just defeated in battle. The musicians of the dead king pass before their conqueror to the number of twenty-eight, of whom seven are players of the nebel (harp), two the flute or double reed-pipe, one the psaltery, and sixteen are singers. Another scene gives us evidence of a secular concert of a most particular kind: the head of the conquered king has been brought back to Nineveh. Ashurbanipal has had it hung from a tree in his park. Seated on a richly decorated couch, he gloats over it as he drinks with his queen, while an orchestra half-hidden behind some foliage adds to his bliss.

Music was not, however, in Assyria or in Chaldea the exclusive privilege of temples and kings. Ctesias recounts that a rich Babylonian, Annarus, when giving a banquet, brought together to amuse his guests an ensemble of 150 women, who sang and played the flute, the harp, and the psaltery. In Egyptian painting and sculpture from the Fourth Dynasty on, there are numerous representations of concerts accompanying religious ceremonies and secular entertainments, or escorting notables on their passage to the next life.

Philippe Virey in *The Tomb of Rekhmara* describes for us a funeral concert as it appears in the paintings that adorn the sepulcher of a prefect at El Kab (Eighteenth Dynasty): "The musicians are shown singing in turn. A girl playing the harp begins: *There is perfume in the air! To the Goddess Mâ! The force that is in her acts in me.* . . . Then the song of a girl who is playing the guitar, followed by that of a girl with a drum, then three men sing in unison, while three women beat the measure, then a harpist sings in his turn, and finally a guitarist."

My design is naturally not to trace in detail the evolution of the concert through the ages, which would be tantamount to putting the whole history of music in one chapter. It is sufficient to recall the great antiquity of the subject and its amplitude; after which I shall limit myself to certain salient features and dates.

In Greece in 586 B.C. we see the supreme exaltation of the virtuoso: That year marks the first appearance, at the Pythian games in Delphi, of the solo on the aulos (a double oboe, not a flute) on the theme, already exploited by citharists, of the combat of Apollo and the Python. This "nome" comprises five episodes: 1) Apollo inspects the field of battle; 2) he provokes the Python to fight; 3) the battle, including an imitation of trumpet calls and of the Python gnashing his teeth; 4) the victory of the god; 5) he celebrates his triumph in dancing. Sakadas of Argos, who was to take the prize and give descriptive music its first patent of nobility, played before an immense crowd, standing on a raised platform, dressed in a long tunic embroidered with dots and stars, and over that, a sleeveless mantle, woven in a checkerboard pattern, ornamented with a ribbon border and a fringe.

It is worth noting that the music of the aulos, brilliant and piercing, more accessible to the large public in that it depended on (and achieved) such descriptive effects, represented a regression from the much subtler art of the citharists. This decline in taste was to become greatly accentuated among the Romans.

We have little information on musical life outside the church in the early Christian centuries; not that secular music did not exist, but it was not recorded or codified. Troubadours and minstrels performed in the castles or in the open air, and we know that in the tenth century at the monastery of St. Gall, a great center of sacred music, the monk Tuotilo had the use of a room where he taught the nobles of the countryside how to play musical instruments. As musical iconography developed with its antiphonaries and psalters, scenes of concerts multiplied, some limited to a few players and singers, others showing them in number. There is hardly a chronicle relating a sovereign's entry, a tournament, a princely marriage, which does not describe a more or less important assembly of musicians, sometimes thirty, forty, or fifty oboes, trumpets, and sackbuts making a joyful noise, sometimes delicate ensembles of singers, or players of the portative organ and the "soft instruments" (as were called those instruments with a sweet tone: the harp, the viol, and the lute) playing motets and melodies.

From the fourteenth century, secular concerts, particularly those which take place in an intimate atmosphere, with few performers and few listeners, take an eminent place in fashionable life (read on this subject *The Courtier* by Baldassare Castiglione, and Boccaccio's *Decameron*, etc.). From this time also, so-called "dinner" music progressively attains a level that its social function would not lead one to expect. In the sixteenth century, a banquet was frequently accompanied by a concert of the rarest quality. Here, reproduced by Charles Van den Borren from the *Discorsi* of Massimo Troiano, is the program performed at Munich on the 22nd of February, 1568, during the wedding celebration of Duke William of Bavaria: first, a Battle in eight parts by "Messer Annibale, organist" (undoubtedly the celebrated Annibale Padovano) played by trombones and curved cornetts; with the first course came a concert of various pieces, among them a motet in seven parts by Lassus, played by five "cornetti alti" and two trombones; during the second course, various works in six parts, including a madrigal by Alessandro Striggio for six "tromboni grossi." The strings entered with the third course, playing two motets in six parts, one of them by Cipriano di Rore. For the fourth course, pieces in twelve parts by Annibale Padovano and other composers, with six viole da braccia, five trombones, one curved cornett, and one regal. With the fifth, sixth, and seventh courses there came a mixture of timbres more and more refined, culminating in a piece in twelve parts for three choirs, the first being made up of four viole da gamba, the second of four large recorders, the third of a dolzaina (a kind of cromorne), a bagpipe, a transverse flute, and a muted cornett. And the concert ended with the whole company singing under the direction of Roland de Lassus.

We can see progress since then in the organization of concerts and in their popularization. Their quality, however, could hardly surpass that of these "dinner concerts."

But in the way of organization, the sixteenth century was marked by important innovations. It was in 1570 that the Puy de Musique of Evreux was founded. This puy, or competition, was not the first of its kind, but from the fifth year of its existence it was regularly crowned by two concerts at which prize works were played; and if one considers that Roland de Lassus was made laureate in 1575 and in 1583, one can judge the renown which the institution rapidly acquired.

The same year 1570 marks the foundation of the Academy of Music and of Poetry by Jean-Antoine de Baïf and Thibault de Courville, in which they set out to form "in the manner of the ancients, a company made up of composers, singers, and instrumentalists, as well as honest listeners thereto." The regulations provided for a concert every Sunday lasting "two hours by the clock," for the assessment of dues, and prescribed the number of rehearsals required of the players and the discipline imposed on the listeners—in short, all the mechanism of an association for subscription concerts.

Such associations spread across Europe under different names. The Italian academies were probably the first in date, but we have no precise information on them until the very end of the sixteenth century. In Germany and in German Switzerland they were called *Collegia musica*, the first probably being the one at Torgau, founded in 1568. In the Low Countries, the *Collegium musicum* of Amsterdam received in 1597 the dedication of the second book of Psalms by Sweelinck, and of another collection of the Psalms of David.

The multiplicity of concerts in the seventeenth century defies description. There were private concerts as organized by de la Barre, the organist, by Champion de Chambonnières, by the singer Michel Lambert, by Mlle. de Certain, a well-known harpsichordist, by the famous lutenist Gallot, and others. And there were aubades and serenades offered by the great nobles who kept "bands" of violinists, or mass affairs like that charivari of 700 fifes, oboes, trombones, and drums, accompanied by twenty-four cannon, which in 1671 at Dunkirk "played" fragments of Lully's *Psyche* before Louis XIV. I must also mention those concerts of the highest type, held daily in the churches, sometimes limited to an organ recital, or to one of those curious duels between organists of which the public was so fond (in 1588, Titelouze against Toussaint Lefebvre, for the position of organist in the cathedral of Rouen; in 1608, Frescobaldi against the Chevalier Costantini, etc.), sometimes involving hundreds of choristers and instrumentalists.

The event of the century in this field was the institution of
public, paid concerts, in London, on September 30, 1672.
That day, a notice published by the *London Gazette* announced to music lovers that at four o'clock in the afternoon,
precisely, and on the following days at the same hour, some
excellent musicians could be heard "in the house of Mr. John
Banister, now called the Musick-School, near the George
Tavern at White Friars."

Banister, former first violinist of the royal chamber orchestra and a composer of merit, pursued this enterprise until 1678.
The *Memoires of Musick* of the honorable Roger North tell
us how it functioned: "He procured a large room in White-
fryars, neer the Temple back gate, and made a large raised box
for the musitians, whose modesty required curtaines. The room
was rounded with seats and small tables alehouse fashion. I͐
[one shilling] was the price and call for what you pleased.
There was very good musick, for Banister found means to
procure the best hands in towne, and some voices to come and
performe there . . ."

When Banister had to stop, a music-mad coal merchant,
Thomas Britton, took up the idea. This curious man, who
came from nowhere—he had begun by carrying coal on his
back through the streets to deliver to customers—had acquired
a solid knowledge of chemistry, music, and the occult sciences.
He installed his concerts in the loft over his shop; admission
was free at first, then Britton decided to charge an annual fee
of ten shillings, plus a penny each time for a cup of coffee.
These concerts lasted from 1678 to 1714, and were frequented
by the London élite, who could applaud there the most
popular masters, starting with Handel.

It was also in London a little later that open air concerts, held daily in good weather, were instituted. Those at Vauxhall began in 1732, with singers, an orchestra, and soon an organ, all installed on a terrace around which the audience sauntered. There were others at Ranelagh and at Marylebone; Handel's concertos were often played there, and Handel composed dances and orchestral pieces for performance at such places.

Meanwhile an institution much more important in itself and in its consequences had seen the light of day in Paris—the Concert Spirituel. Anne-Danican Philidor, one of the sons of André Philidor the elder, and a composer of modest merit himself, had had the idea of making an arrangement with the Sieur de Francine, Lully's heir, and by this fact, titulary of a privilege which gave him the exclusive license "to cause to be sung any entire piece of music, in French verse or any other tongue."

Philidor obtained from Francine, for a sum, the authorization to present in Paris, for three years, concerts of "chapel music" on those thirty-five or so days of the year when the observance of religious festivals suspended performances at the Opéra. The inaugural concert took place on March 18, 1725, in a room in the Tuileries decorated by Bérain, with a program which included two motets by Delalande, the *Christmas Concerto* by Corelli, and some violin solos. The enterprise was an immediate success and lasted until the end of the eighteenth century. When he renewed his lease in 1727, Philidor obtained the right to add to the concerts given on religious holidays, two weekly sessions during the winter and one during the summer, at which secular as well as sacred music was played. After that, secular cantatas, sonatas, and concertos for all instruments alternated with motets for large choirs; and virtuosos from all countries vied for the honor of appearing at the Concert Spirituel, which achieved a European reputation, so that foreign capitals, Vienna, Amsterdam, London, etc., were inspired by its organization to create their own concert societies.

From this time on, the subject becomes definitely too vast and involved to lend itself to a summary which would be anything more than a simple enumeration. Public concerts multiplied, less however than private concerts, recitals by virtuosos, and chamber music sessions. What is of prime interest now is not to number them, but to try to understand their real significance, to grasp, if possible, the fluctuations of taste to which they correspond. The study to undertake would be that of their musical content. It would be fascinating to clear the underbrush from a number of paths more or less entangled and confused; to see in what measure the growing austerity of programming and of style of execution marks an improvement over the eccentricities and curiosities that were the rage among Mozart's contemporaries and over the bravura that was accepted up to the beginning of the last century and was the rule thereafter (the concerts of Chopin, of Liszt, of Paganini!); to see if the growing split between the ever more rapid refinement of the composers' technique and the degree of initiation of the public is not on the way to engendering an immense misunderstanding of concerts; to see finally, if in a period of unregulated acceleration, in which music exhausts itself in trying to reflect the times, its true vocation should not rather be to help us find an escape.

III

The Conductor

FOR THE newcomer in a concert hall, the spectacle of a
conductor in action is mysterious. It remains so for a certain number of habitual concert-goers; and this is understandable, given the complexity and strangeness of the gestures
by which this dictator expresses himself, and even more when
one observes that at the head of the same orchestra and in the
presence of the same work, several conductors succeeding each
other will have almost totally different gestures. What, then, is
the secret link between them, to what common discipline do
they refer, to what necessity do they answer?

The question is not so naive as one might be tempted to
think: not only are certain virtuosos of the baton "illegible"
except for those musicians accustomed to playing under their
direction (when they conduct others, they are obliged to
simplify their manner), but there are those whose technique
defies analysis even by other conductors. I remember that
when Furtwängler came several times to perform with his
Berlin Philharmonic, none of his Parisian colleagues of the
time, not even Monteux, could explain the way in which, by a
sort of vibrato of the baton incomprehensible to the uninitiated
observer, he obtained stops and starts of a lightning precision.

Be it understood that I shall not try here to draw up a new

Art of Directing the Orchestra after Wagner, Berlioz, Wein-
gartner, Schünemann, and other luminaries. I shall limit myself
to the external demonstrations of the conductor on his podium
during the concert.

There is a general theory, hardly necessary to recall, that
assigns different roles to the two hands. The right, which holds
the baton, beats the time; the left indicates everything else, the
nuances and accents, the entry of the various instruments, the
disposition of the banks of sound, etc. This postulates a complete independence of the two arms in relation to each other,
attained in practice only by the privileged few.

You may convince yourself of this by observing carefully
those conductors imprudent enough to dispense with the
baton, seduced by a certain theatrical manner of kneading the
sounds, of working the orchestra, with the palms reversed, the
thumbs like a spatula, and the little finger coquettishly crooked
the whole time. While the tempo stays moderate, the two
hands maintain their theoretical independence; as soon as it
quickens, right and left hand start to beat with a symmetry
the length of the baton is not there to hide. (There is an excellent illustration of this in the film *Carnegie Hall,* when
Artur Rodzinski appears in the allegro movement of a symphony, during almost all of which he saves half his effort by
putting his left hand in his pocket, since it would only be
doing the same work as the right.)

This parenthesis closed, let us remark that the division of
work between the two hands is not and should not be rigorous.
With the arm that beats time an experienced conductor, without curtailing that role in the least, can obtain a quantity of
expressive directions by modifying the intensity, the vivacity,

and the orientation of his movements.

But for us spectators, the problem remains: how explain, in the same musical situation, both the frantic agitation of one conductor and the quasi-immobility of another?

To my mind, this can be done by attributing three sources to their movements, or better, three categories of intentions:

1. Certain movements are meant for the orchestra.
2. Certain movements are meant for the public.
3. Some concern only the conductor, corresponding to a personal necessity I shall discuss later.

1. As for the first category, I direct my reader to the treatises on theory, underlining especially a most ingenious proposition put forth by Lazare Saminsky in Henry Prunières's *Revue Musicale* (November 1922): "Our field of vision embraces not only the objects we fix on and on which our visual axes converge, but also those placed at a certain distance which we distinguish by a sort of lateral vision." And Saminsky goes on to say in substance that the instrumentalist attentively directs his eyes to the music, but, thanks to his lateral vision, he perceives the directions of the conductor by a subconscious effort. So that these directions may be perceived with the least expense of conscious attention, without effort of will, it is necessary "that the rhythmic action of the conductor should have a certain center, a hearth, so to speak, from which it radiates; and it must displace itself only in very narrow limits, so that the instrumentalists can always have it in their lateral field of vision. Nothing is more absurd than a conductor who marks the rhythm with both hands, or who changes his place

constantly, thereby exacting from the musicians an expense of conscious energy which is entirely unnecessary."

2. The gestures meant for the public are not all directed to the same end. Some, in the mind of the conductor, tend to help the listener penetrate the sense of what is being played for him. Some, still in the mind of the conductor, if the latter has in him the actor's vocation more or less repressed, have for their object a display of his originality, of the profundity of his thought, of the ardor of his temperament, or the elegance of his plastic form.

Except in certain special cases, when for example the conductor in question has been in the movies where he could indulge himself in bad acting to his heart's content, one has a duty to show self-restraint in diagnosing the reason why a conductor imitates an Iberian dance, with back arched and hand on hip, to express the *Alborada del Gracioso*, or sometimes acts out, on the two square meters of his podium, the drama a symphony suggests to him—a symphony to which the composer did not add the least bit of descriptive commentary.

The cultivated public has not much to gain from such "enlightenments." On the other hand, there is no doubt that those people, rather numerous, who go to concerts for extra-musical reasons, find in them an element of distraction that counts in the final success, which is composed, as we know, of the sum total of applause, regardless of source.

3. The third source of movements deserves more than cursory notes. Here is the gist of it.

What I have to say does not concern those great conductors whose interpretations are constantly controlled by the most lucid intelligence. There are others not less eminent whose main characteristic is a hypersensitivity which puts them, while they are conducting, into a sort of mediumistic state, or trance, with marvelous artistic results if they have the technique, the intuition, and also the instinctive critical sense to put a brake on their internal demon (if not, disaster, which we have too often witnessed!).

But, as their nervous tension mounts, these emotional types need a release, a way to get rid of energy, without consideration of either orchestra or public, just like the child I see dancing on the beach, drunk with the triple enchantment of sea, sun, and wind. I have the impression that Furtwängler's convulsive vibrato was often nothing but this, and it should not be confused with the gesture by which the conductor traditionally calls on the violins for a vibrato.

The case is often the same with Munch. He used to get some exercise by swinging both arms laterally, in a parallel movement. Recently he has affected a kind of circular movement of the arms, like a circus rider.

One day I asked one of the musicians how the orchestra reacted to such moments. "You mean when he begins to play the fool? . . ." I do not believe Munch will take offense at this anecdote. It was said with such an air of amused indulgence, even complicity, by a man who had just manifested such admiration, enthusiasm, and affection for his chief, that one could not suspect an intention to criticize. It was simply the acknowledgment by the orchestra of that phenomenon I have tried to indicate: this part of the motion is not meant for the players, but permits the conductor to discharge an exhausting overload of nervous energy. And though it does not much concern the public, the latter takes an untoward interest in it, because of the monkeyshines it stimulates on the part of second-rate conductors.

Sometimes Munch, in the heat of a great romantic development, passes his baton back and forth from his right hand to his left. I have seen a very naive imitator deliver himself of this transfer twenty times and more in a single movement of a symphony. But this brings up back to category number 2, in which it is less sympathetic; and perhaps I have said enough to show, as I leave it, the complexity of my subject.

Yet I have reserved the most delicate element, the very center of the mystery—a certain action of the conductor independent of any gesture, a certain telepathy thanks to which the whole orchestra at the same time espouses his thought.

This power has been questioned. I think it can be no more denied in the case of the great inspired conductors than it can in the case of such virtuosos as Paderewski, Ysaÿe, Casals, Enesco—each capable, on his good days, of casting a spell over the auditorium, orchestra and audience alike, from the first chord or the first stroke of the bow. What is certain is that the study of this phenomenon remains to be done.

BRUNO WALTER

I expect that this section will displease at least one reader: the one who wrote me not long ago to reproach me for wasting paper on performers when there is so much to be said about the works of music.

I do not think, like him, that the works have such need of our services. The best-known are weighed down under a mass of glosses. On those new works which we review after one hearing, we shed but a feeble light, for want of time for reflection and for lack of space in the specialized reviews. And is it not of interest to catch on the wing the virtuoso, who is by definition fleeting, and whose vanished traits later historians would try in vain to recall without the aid of contemporary accounts?

Whereas the works endure. On coming back to them, one even finds them clarified, thanks to the work of assimilation that has gone on in the depths of the subconscious (thus was I sure, on a second hearing, that the *Three Dances* by Duruflé ranks with the most ambitious symphonic poems and ought to remain in the repertory; thus shall I know only after another encounter whether a certain Overture in C major is as narrowly derived from Wagner's *Meistersinger* as it presently seems to me to be). Finally, and I repeat myself deliberately, interpretation, at a certain level of achievement, *is* creation. For example, when Bruno Walter was the interpreter.

As seen by a deaf man, Bruno Walter would not have seemed to offer a rare spectacle. He did nothing many other illustrious conductors do not do. Little inclined formerly to act out his scores, he was in his later years still more sparing of external effects. He did not play the tragedian. No objurgations, ecstasies, or threats, no palms reversed, no prancing, no pirouetting. He did not carry the weight of a hundred instrumentalists at the end of his arm. He did not stroke the side of some imaginary urn with an unctuous left hand. His baton was a baton: not a sceptre, not a paint brush, not a hatchet, not a horsewhip. He did not abandon it in the andante to let the soft benediction of his right hand float over the violas. Long would be the list of all that he repudiated as tending to inflame those people who look more than they listen.

But for those who listen and look as a musician does, what richness, and above all, what clarity!

As opposed to Furtwängler, who was also a conductor of the first rank but who could only be followed by an orchestra instructed in his code, Bruno Walter had an immediate "readability." His right arm beat the measure or its accents in all simplicity. Once the music was launched, unless the tempo had to be modified, the path of the baton was restrained almost to immobility. No less soberly the left hand assumed its customary task: to indicate the entrances, regulate the intensities, balance the sections. In truth, the essential element of his work was the glance that accompanied it, carrying multiple injunctions that other conductors externalize at the price of an agitation of the four limbs projected to the four winds.

The magnetism of this look, the extraordinary power that it carried, could be measured by the instantaneous reaction of the orchestra, which immediately became a coherent whole. Even more than by its brilliance in the virtuoso passages (a Haydn finale!) one was struck by the way the thirty violins of the string section shaped a melody as a free and inspired singer would. This quality of vocal improvisation was manifested from the beginning in the *Oxford Symphony;* it transfigured the *Siegfried Idyll,* which we used to find somewhat long-drawn-out, with its two themes taken up again and again without notable transformations. Without transformations? Bruno Walter, playing the text with infinite respect, made all the possible expressions of tenderness and hope succeed one another.

The magic again operated in the Brahms Second Symphony.

If confirmed anti-Brahmsians found it neither heavy nor diffuse, it was not that Bruno Walter betrayed it or rewrote it. His secret consisted in dominating the long construction from a position high enough to clarify its large lines, in not confounding depth with slowness, in animating the developments when they started to sound academic, in softening the basses when something interesting was taking place over them, and in refusing to install himself behind that opaque *grisaille* that is adopted by some as representing Brahmsian sonority par excellence.

This symphony, at the conclusion of the concert, earned for the conductor and the orchestra of the Société des Concerts du Conservatoire an ovation comparable to that invariably unleashed by *Scheherazade*, Ravel's *Boléro*, or *The Ride of the Valkyries*.

Which proves that Brahms, as we know, is in large measure slandered: which proves that Bruno Walter made music like no one else.

FURTWÄNGLER

Furtwängler's return to Paris after the Second World War was the more remarkable because it was announced with a certain reserve, as if unfavorable reactions were to be feared. That would have been most unjust. Wagner's granddaughter Friedelind, who grew up in the heart of the German musical world under Hitlerism, has given us a portrait of the great conductor that is certainly lacking in goodwill (she was a partisan of Toscanini, and the two maestros were not overfond of one another). But even she tells us nothing about her compatriot that would make him hateful as a man; and more to the point, nothing that should have dissuaded us from going to applaud the musician.

Such was the judgment of the public at the Théâtre des Champs-Elysées, where the same concert, with the Fifth Symphony of Beethoven, two *Nocturnes* (*Nuages-Fêtes*) of Debussy, *Till Eulenspiegel* by Strauss, the Prelude to *Tristan*, and the *Liebestod*, was repeated three times to a sold-out house.

Traditional this program may have been, but cut to measure. We had wonderful memories of the *Nocturnes* and of *Tristan* under Furtwängler's baton. But whatever he might present, how could we not be anxious to know the direction of his evolution in the ten years that had elapsed?

Add to that a particular curiosity: what would be his effect on an orchestra not his own?

There is much mystery in the art of conducting, and technically speaking, he was always the most enigmatic of conductors. At the head of the Berlin Philharmonic he had his own way of making it start and stop. His right arm, with a flourish, began a series of oscillations, a sort of vibrato, in the middle of which (not at the beginning or the end) the orchestra came in with the precision of a chronometer; and in the middle of a similar vibrato they all stopped, as one man, on one chord. In the interval his gestures were hardly more readable. The best qualified of his colleagues never could analyze them; only the players followed them without apparent difficulty.

Would it be the same with instrumentalists he was going to conduct for the first time? It was evident at once that he had simplified his manner, adapting himself to the circumstances, but also that his profound personality had mellowed, become more serene.

In the agitations for which his critics formerly reproached him, there was perhaps one part spectacle, not necessarily voluntary. Although Friedelind, as a child of thirteen, observed that in the pit at Bayreuth where the orchestra was out of sight, he did not practice his "usual gymnastics," that implies not that these gymnastics were an imposture when he gave himself over to them in full view of an audience, but that he was swayed then by the predilection which listener-spectators show for conductors who "externalize."

But on this occasion we found him delivered from this temptation. In sovereign isolation from us he made music with his instrument of one hundred voices, the magnificent orchestra of the Société des Concerts. He made himself easily understood, less by his gestures than by his extraordinary power of suggestion. The musicians observed the principal injunctions of his baton, and wisely ignored the extras which risked leading them into error through lack of familiarity (which explains a short hesitation in the Andante of the Fifth at the first concert). One can admit that a part of the superfluous movement —as for example when he beat all the eighth notes of a melodic line—was not addressed to the orchestra. It was (see above) an overflowing of musical emotion that was thus expressed, a way of tracing for himself the contours of the work being interpreted.

Furtwängler's hypersensitivity naturally accomplished marvels in the *Nocturnes* and *Tristan*, different as they are in style. He surprised me more in the Fifth, which people of my age had heard too often to hope to find there any still undiscovered beauty. He positively re-created it through his fidelity to the text, in moderating the tempo of the first movement, notably in the famous passage for basses in the scherzo, in lightening the developments and bringing out the dialogues of the woodwinds that one never hears, in highlighting the contrasts, in giving the trumpets in the finale the éclat of a Wagnerian fanfare. This alliance of so clear an intellectual conception with the sort of trance-like quality that never left him seems to me to have been the perfect realization of the interpreter's art.

KOUSSEVITZKY

Serge Koussevitzky had an extraordinarily full life. His career had something of the fairy-tale about it. Picture to yourself a little boy, son of a humble musician in Vichny-Volotsk in the province of Tver, who is haunted, as far back as his memories go, by the dream of someday conducting an orchestra. One of his favorite games is to line up the chairs in the dining room of his house, put a desk in front of them, and then act out the conductor's entrance, his mounting the podium, his bow to the audience, his lifted arm, the symphony which he unleashes.

At the age of seven he has an opportunity to direct a small ensemble in a composition of his own making. But he has to think of a surer career. Soon he will adopt an instrument which is seldom chosen, the double bass, will master its technique, will attain a virtuosity which will make him the successor of the Dragonettis and the Bottesinis of old. But for all that he does not forget his first ambition. In Berlin, where he goes to finish his studies at the Hochschule, he follows avidly the concerts of Nikisch, score in hand.

And here the dream comes true. His fame has grown, he is engaged the world over as a virtuoso; in 1905 he marries Nathalia Ouchakova, the daughter of one of the richest merchants in Russia. On the wedding day his future father-in-law asks him what he would like to receive as a wedding gift. The reply: "A great symphony orchestra!" Although surprised, the excellent man acquiesces; recruiting is begun; in 1907 the Concerts Koussevitzky enter the musical life of Moscow.

From that time on, Koussevitzky's life was too active and had too many ramifications to lend itself to a summary, however brief. He continued for a time to appear as an instrumentalist. I was present at one of his concerts in the old Salle Pleyel in which the keystone was a Concerto for Viola d'Amore and Double Bass, composed from all appearances by Henri Casadesus, but attributed for greater prestige to Antonio Lorenziti. From his bass with its beautiful dark varnish and its long neck—in reality more of a large bass viol—he drew velvety tones and passage work as agile as that of the viola d'amore, and which, thanks to its harmonics, reached just as high in the upper register.

But his principal activities centered around the direction of the orchestra. From 1910 on, he undertook tours of symphonic concerts, with soloists like Scriabin, in cities along the Volga which were almost totally without musical resources. In Moscow he produced Scriabin's *Prometheus*, for orchestra, choirs, piano, organ, and color organ! and Prokofiev's *Scythian Suite*. In 1913 he invited Debussy to come to conduct an entire program of his works. Between times he had founded in Berlin, in 1909, the Editions Russes de Musique, a publishing firm to propagate the music of his compatriots. Thus he established, without official concurrence, a double current of exchanges.

Installed in Paris after the Russian Revolution, from 1921 on he produced concerts at the Opéra, for which he assembled an élite orchestra, composed of the best elements of our great concert associations, and which created a sensation. But it was in the United States, at the head of the Boston Symphony Orchestra, that he accomplished his greatest task. Monteux, who preceded him, had left him a choice instrument. He continued to perfect it, and especially enlarged the repertory by commissioning scores from the greatest composers of the time. The French were high on the list. In 1923 in Paris he had introduced Ravel's transcription of Mussorgsky's *Pictures at an Exhibition*. Boston was to owe to him the world première of the Suite in F and the Third Symphony by Roussel, works by Messiaen and by Darius Milhaud, and the First Symphony of Honegger, whose Fifth Symphony, also commissioned by him, he was not to have the pleasure of directing. He welcomed scores from the young Russian school, Obouhov, Lourié, Nabokov, as well as from Stravinsky and Prokofiev, and all the heads of contemporary schools, Bartók, Schoenberg, Hindemith, Villa-Lobos, Malipiero, Martinu, Britten, Tansman. As for the United States, we know what Roy Harris, Samuel Barber, Aaron Copland, Walter Piston, and William Schuman owe to him.

The last two concerts Koussevitzky conducted in Paris gave us an opportunity to proclaim again what a master conductor he was. The great instinctive conductor of the early years had become a refined technician. But his magnetism remained

intact; his ascendancy over the musicians resulted as much
from their respect for the sum of his experience, which they
acknowledged from the first, as from the sympathy he radi-
ated and which established between them and him immediate
contact, a reciprocal confidence.

IV

Child Prodigies

EACH APPEARANCE on the concert stage of a particularly precocious virtuoso brings back into circulation a certain number of ready-made ideas on the subject of child prodigies. One of the most common consists in treating them like one homogeneous body, all cut on a single model, and destined to the ephemeral fate of a display of fireworks: a brief flare-up, some delayed sparks, and then nothing.

It is true that one witnesses in concerts, from time to time, the exhibition of poor, overworked, enervated, pitiable children, simple objects of curiosity whose success is used up once their date of birth can no longer reasonably be falsified. The least disinherited of these young old men and women then try for the Conservatory, and in the most favorable outcome, emerge with a second prize, won through seniority.

But this is one category among others, and the least numerous. No other art, in reality, offers so many examples of precocity as music. Goethe, in his *Conversations with Eckermann*, finds the explanation in that music is "something innate and interior in us, which does not ask to be nourished or informed by life." Perhaps. It is certain that most of the children whose maturity disconcerts us obey an inner necessity, a vocation it would be vain, even dangerous, to deny. There is no apparent norm in the birth and development of this vocation.

With some it is a sort of game; others become suddenly solemn, as if inspired from on high, the moment music takes hold of them. Some begin by playing an instrument; others by improvising; others have several talents. Often one of the gifts recedes along the route, or there is a criss-cross, the presumed composer becoming a virtuoso, the apprentice virtuoso a composer.

How numerous are they? So many that the word "prodigy" should, in the final count, be abandoned. Without having undertaken a methodical census, I have come across hundreds of them since the end of the seventeenth century (that is the time when biographers began to pride themselves on their accuracy), and, among them, names of the greatest distinction. Not only those masters who have been made widely known under their youthful aspect in the popularized biographies: Lully, Mozart, Liszt, but also J. S. Bach, Purcell, Handel, who was an organist at the age of eight, Rameau, an accomplished harpsichordist at seven, Haydn, Beethoven, advertised at seven and a half as "a boy of six years," although he was sufficiently extraordinary without this trickery, and Weber, Schubert, Mendelssohn, Schumann, who wrote from the time he was seven, Brahms at ten, and Rossini, at that age helping his parents teach music, soon afterwards singing in the theater, accompanying, playing the horn, and Chopin, Franck, Bizet, Saint-Saëns, Albéniz, who made his début on the podium at the age of four; and those who made their official début at a normal age, but who had already darkened some doors during their spare time in their school days: Grieg, Chabrier, Rimsky, Borodin, and others, without forgetting those who were less well known for their precocity: Telemann, Roman, Strungk, Clementi, Gossec, Grétry, Philodor, Hummel, Paer, Dussek, Field, Hérold, Stephen Heller, Meyerbeer, who, at the age of six, shone as a pianist at amateur concerts in Berlin, and others by the dozens.

There are many more among musicians who have made a career as virtuosos. By running through the list of their names, we can draw some useful conclusions.

The cultivation of the child prodigy is not, as some have pretended, an invention of our feverish times, avid for profit, in a hurry to turn even future promise into money. The court of Louis XIV celebrated a five-year-old violinist, Antoine Forqueray, harpsichordists of the same age, Dandrieu and Daquin, and Elizabeth Jacquet, an organist-harpsichordist and composer at the age of nine. In Italy, Germany, and England, as in France, from that time on many violinists who were later outstanding began their tours between seven and ten years of age, or had a permanent place in an orchestra.

Precocious virtuosos were not and are not now destined to a premature death. This can be the lot of some unlucky ones or those who are too much exploited. What became of Maria Brochard, who in 1835 at the age of five, improvised and transposed? Of Rosa de Baraibar, who in 1854, was four and a half years old, and not only "played like Liszt at ten years" but sang with exquisite taste? And of Pilar Osorio, who in 1910, aged three years, played, according to the review *S.I.M.*, "the most difficult pieces on a piano scaled to her size" . . . ? As to Pepito Arriola, who gave his first concert at the age of three, swallowed in three months almost all musical theory, and composed at three and a half, it is certain that he did not hold this pace for long. Others fell by the wayside, or abandoned their career. But the deans of the profession are almost all former child prodigies; I cite only Viotti, Spohr, Joachim, Auer, Hubay, Clara Schumann, and Francis Planté, who lived to be almost a hundred.

It is not true that child prodigies exhaust their capital of talent for their mature years by dipping into it when they are young. Witness the artists already named, and other leading talents of the stature of Paganini, Vieuxtemps, Wieniawski, Sivori, Anton Rubinstein, Teresa Carreño, Busoni. Shall I recall the most precocious of all of them, William Crotch? At two years and three weeks (this happened in 1777), he discovered on the organ, guided only by his instinct, the harmonization of *God Save the King*, which did not prevent him from becoming one of the principal musicians of the kingdom and the director of the Royal Academy of Music.

But let us look around us: Kreisler played the violin at the age of four; at ten, Marcel Dupré could play the great organs of Rouen, and Yves Nat direct a symphonic work of his own composition; Aline Van Barentzen, Yvonne Lefébure, Ginette Neveu appeared in public at an age when most girls are playing with dolls and hoops. And we are familiar with the débuts of Heifetz, Elman, and Menuhin.

Finally, such a development of the musical sense is in no way prejudicial to the other intellectual and artistic disciplines. Witness again the names cited above: they include perhaps two or three players restricted to the practice of their instrument, but, at their side, theorists of music, philosophers, critics, mathematicians, chemists, letter writers capable of expressing themselves elegantly in three or four languages. Anyone who studied them from this angle would probably be well paid for his trouble.

They do not much resemble each other, even in their behavior.

The first to make a great impression on me was Mischa Elman, in 1906, at the Queen's Hall in London, in the Brahms Concerto. He seemed a little gone to seed, with his hairy calves, big for the twelve years that his publicity gave him. In reality, he was almost fifteen, but from what one heard, he had long ago reached this stupefying plateau of technique and sonorous amplitude. What was striking in his countenance was an air of unbeatable self-confidence, an intrepidity, as he faced the orchestra, of a lion-tamer before wild beasts; on the other hand, a complete submission to the public, which he saluted by bowing almost to the ground, in the oriental manner, supple as a sponge.

How different was Menuhin at his Paris début, at the Concerts Lamoureux. I had the privilege of attending his first rehearsal. He came on the stage, in a white sweater, so childlike, so natural, that the first violinist, in whom the appearance of another violinist had always provoked an expression of ill humor impossible to hide, smiled at him and took his violin in order to tune it. Yehudi placidly acquiesced; then, the instrument tuned, took it back and thanked him. Then he played. From the first note, a thrill of excitement ran through the orchestra, including the first violinist. Menuhin seemed to accomplish without effort a task agreeable above all others. When he had finished, he left the stage just as calm, as natural, as when he came on, ready to take up again his normal life of a small boy like the others.

With Ruth Slenczynski, things seemed less simple. She was seven years old when she was first heard here, and had already performed several unusual exploits: first scales at sixteen months on a toy piano, first real lesson at three and a half years, first concert at four. In repose, her appearance was truly childish: tall as three apples, but thickset, with good red cheeks, laughing black eyes, and a charming vivacity. At the piano she was metamorphosed, her fixed look and concentration of thought made more noticeable by a slight squint which was not otherwise present. One could not help but think of a reincarnation. But while the boy Menuhin evoked Mozart at that age, Ruth might rather have given asylum to the demoniac soul of a virtuoso like Paganini, or, at other times, to one of the early polyphonists. She had two chosen domains: either works of a supertechnique which she mastered with a sort of wild gaiety, or contrapuntal music, in which she moved with the ease of a Ferruccio Busoni. I have seen her learn in five or six mornings the Bach *Chromatic Fantasy and Fugue*. On the other hand, a simple melody of Schumann, Chopin, or Grieg left her indifferent, and she played it like a schoolgirl. In this case, her attitude at the piano was that of a schoolgirl, whereas, confronted with pages that she loved, she paled, and entered that second state I spoke of, remaining there as long as her fingers stayed in contact with the keyboard. When she took them away, her face resumed its normal expression that very instant. All this happened as if there had been a sharp break in the current.

Tamara Obolenska appeared in Paris toward her thirteenth spring. She was much less talked about than Menuhin or even Ruth Slenczynski—justly so, if tangible results are what count.

She and her mother had, I think, emigrated from Russia, and they led a difficult life, very dignified, with too perfect a scorn for the strategy which leads to success. The girl's character was undecipherable. Smiling, but silent, with a glacial politeness, she worked as she liked, and maternal chidings could not move her. If one asked her to play before someone who might further her career, she usually did it with the worst will in the world. It was she, condescending, who seemed to examine the examiner. A great pianist, Alfred Cortot, who had been brought to hear her one day, departed furious, proclaiming that he knew dozens of aspiring pianists who were more remarkable; the demonstration that she had just given deserved no better. But, in the weeks that followed, she gave a recital that left us gasping in admiration; an easy, sparkling virtuosity, with a fullness and variety of tone obtained only by the few elect. She was one of those performers who are lifted out of themselves by the presence of the public.

Meanwhile she obtained her first prize at the Conservatory. She performed in public again several times. In defiance of the most elementary rules of publicity, she appeared each time under a new name: Tamara Obolenska, then Tamara Lenska, then simply Tamara. One wondered how many syllables would be left at the next concert. Then it was said that she had abandoned the piano for the dance. But there she took only a second prize: they had made that fierce individualist perform in a *pas de deux!*

I heard her again the next year by chance at a gala, a pianist once again, and of the first rank. A definitive return? Or simply an interlude before a third vocation?

No, child prodigies are not all cut from the same cloth.

YEHUDI MENUHIN

On February 6, 1927, Yeduhi Menuhin made his Paris début at the Concerts Lamoureux. I have already recounted how the orchestra, composed of men of experience, gave a start of surprise and admiration, when the little boy, all simplicity and goodness, who had so graciously handed his three-quarter Grandino to the first violinist to check the tuning, attacked the Allegro of the *Symphonie Espagnole*. Sonority, rhythm, technique, and maturity of style exceeded anything one could have imagined. Word of mouth publicity did its work. Printed criticism was more cautious for a time: too many near-prodigies had abused its good nature. Robert Kemp, who signed himself R. Dézarnaux in *Liberté* (February 8, 1927), was so solidly ranged against child prodigies that he saw nothing more in Menuhin than the equivalent—at ten years of age to be sure—of a good second prize at the Conservatory!

Still, at the next concert, Menuhin had to turn people away. There was a great curiosity to see him; legends were already springing up. I had the idea of seeking information directly from his father, who cooperated with good grace.

When he received me, in their furnished apartment on the Rue de Sèvres, the boy was working on a concerto by Spohr. He was polishing the details with a wise lack of haste. It was explained to me that when he was at work, no one, not even a member of his family, was allowed to enter his room. And here is what I learned about his childhood, over a sonorous background of music that the Spohr continued to furnish.

Yehudi Menuhin came into the world in New York, his

father said, on January 22, 1917, of American parents of
Russian origin on his father's side, Tartar on his mother's. Here
I should note, regretfully, that his father, yielding to current
custom, took nine months off Yehudi's age, since he was actually born on April 22, 1916. The erroneous date of January
22, 1917, continued to appear in print for a time, up to and
including Schmidl's conscientious dictionary (Vol. III, 1938).
Later when the information came directly from Yehudi, the
exact date was immediately established. In fact, one of the
dominant traits of his character is an intransigeant love of the
truth. In his own comments on himself there is neither com-
placency nor false modesty. I can remember asking him during
the intermission of a concert toward his eleventh or twelfth
year if he tried to write music. An affirmative reply. And
when would we hear it? Reply: "When it is as good as Beethoven's."

To get back to his childhood. He was nine months old when
the family moved to San Francisco; he was fourteen months
old when his parents, who wanted to go to a concert and had
no one to leave the baby with, decided to take him with them,
resigned in advance to leaving the auditorium if he cried.
Menuhin himself told of this experience in an article published
in 1933 in the *Courrier Musical:*

They wrapped me in a large shawl and filled a bottle with milk;
if I cried, they said to themselves, they would try to quiet me with
the milk; if I continued to cry, my mother would take me out of
the concert hall for a minute; and if I continued to resist the
music, they would be forced to take me home and miss the rest of
the concert. The experiment was a great success. I did not cry
at all, they tell me; I thrust aside the shawl, ignored the milk, and

became completely absorbed in the music.

From that day on, I was an habitué of the concert hall. I formed the habit of noticing the various instruments and choosing the performers I liked best. At the age of four, I said I wanted violin lessons from the first violinist, Louis Persinger. My parents were amused. It had never entered their heads that their son could be a sort of musical prodigy. They wanted me to be an ordinary child, drinking plenty of milk, playing in the fresh air, and not bothering my head with such things as the study of music. But I had an entirely different idea, and as I had always had the habit of expressing my views with absolute clarity, I continued until the day one of the teachers who worked for my father bought me a violin as a toy. At first I was enchanted, but my joy cooled rapidly when I discovered that I could produce nothing similar to the sounds which I heard at concerts. I was so angry that I broke the violin, and to the great annoyance of my parents, I took up my campaign again and demanded a real violin, such as I heard at concerts.

Soon after, they consented to buy him a real violin and to give him a teacher, Sigmund Anker. At five years and two months, he started lessons with Louis Persinger; at the end of eight months, the pupil was heard with the San Francisco Symphony Orchestra in the Mendelssohn Concerto. Then came the successes in New York, then the début in Paris.

In France he worked under the direction of Georges Enesco, the work consisting especially in reading the classics together and in completing a musical education already well advanced.

Here we should stop to measure his father's influence. If Yehudi's personality has indeed developed so fully, he owes it to a way of life many parents of precocious children would do well to follow. Here are the outlines:

—The amount of time devoted to the study of the violin proportioned to the age and the strength of the child: in 1926, two and a half hours a day; in 1927, three hours.

—The study of music extended, at the age of nine, to harmony, then to counterpoint, orchestration, and the history of music, completed by listening to the best records, attending the best concerts and chamber music recitals.

—A preponderant place accorded to general education, through lessons given at home to the boy and his sisters by teachers of English, French, and German, their father teaching them history and mathematics himself.

—The inviolability of the time set aside for games, sports, reading, and family life.

—No contact with journalists, photographers, men of the world: outside of his work and his concerts, Yehudi lived like any other child of his age.

—Only a limited number of engagements accepted for him; at the start, one a year; two a year when he was nine, then, up to adolescence, one a week at the most, during three months of the year, the rest of the time being devoted to work without pressure, and several times—for example, in 1927 after his Paris début, and in 1928 after the memorable performance of the Beethoven Concerto in New York—a year's retreat, without any, or few, public appearances.

But I can do no better than to reproduce a long note written by the senior Mr. Menuhin for the press at the end of 1929 in which he comments on the education of Yehudi and his two sisters, and explains his pedagogical ideas and the sacrifices he consented to, with a pride that is somewhat naive but after all most legitimate. Here is the text, with the most significant passages reproduced *in extenso,* the rest simply summarized.

On December 12, 1927, Yehudi Menuhin made his last appearance in Carnegie Hall, New York. Since then, with the exception of his homecoming San Francisco concerts in January and February, one with the San Francisco Symphony and the other in recital, each time playing to an audience of ten or eleven thousand in the San Francisco Civic Auditorium, Yehudi made no other public appearances. On January 6, 1928, we left New York for San Francisco. We left behind us all the commercial offers, glories, and glamors, with their glaring inducements, and while yet on the train homeward bound, began to map out our plans for a year of work, study, growth, and recreation for our three children. Again, just as after Yehudi's triumphant appearance in Paris, a principle was rigidly laid down: No more public engagements for at least ten months! We have lived up to our own principle without experiencing the least difficulty in conquering temptation. There were enough offers during this period to make us rich within three or four months; instead we borrowed a little to supplement our funds in order to square our budget.

Newspapermen, photographers, and the commercial atmosphere of New York had to give way to a healthy, normal home atmosphere. Our home had to house a school for our three children, a conservatory where the three of them could practice simultaneously, and a playhouse. We the parents had to be at once parents and teachers instead of tourists and managers of Yehudi's business affairs.

A staff of eight teachers, each one a specialist in his or her own subject but with a solid general background behind it, was at once engaged to look after our three children at our own home. Each one comes in from two to four times during each week. We parents act more in the capacity of directors, advisers, substitutes, and playmates. We have two French teachers for the girls and Yehudi, the sisters Godchaux—probably the most cultured family in our community; two piano teachers for the two girls (lately we have one piano teacher for the two of them, Mr. Lev Schorr); one violin master, Mr. Louis Persinger; one harmony teacher for Yehudi, Mr. J. Paterson; one English teacher, a professor at the University of California, Mr. Arnold Perstein, for Yehudi, and one English teacher, Mrs. Perstein, for the girls; one German teacher, Mr. Collinger, of Stanford University, the latest addition to our staff of teachers. In addition, arithmetic and history are my own subjects—history, because I am interested in giving our children a liberal and humanistic interpretation and analysis of, and attitude to, life past and present.

All business talk, interviews and correspondence about Yehudi's next year's affairs, inquiries and correspondence from all the continents of the earth, had to be on principle carried on outside the home, or at night when the children were asleep.

There follows a paragraph concerning the only exception to the decision taken to suspend all professional activity: Yehudi would make a certain number of records for the Victor Talking Machine Co. He would do it as much out of duty as for pleasure: "The harder the task, the more interesting," is his motto.

Next the press release analyzes the daily schedule: the noon hours from 12:30 to 3:00 P.M. during the week, and all day Sunday, rest, walks, and sports. "Practice, study, reading, and recreation were carefully and proportionally allotted so as to balance one another, and never to thwart the physical progress of the children."

As to concerts, the whole family would go to the best of those taking place in the afternoon. If there were exceptional concerts in the evening, Yehudi would go with his parents. Recorded music from a large repertory of classic and modern works accompanied meals. "The biggest punishment one can invent for our children is to say, 'This morning we shall break-fast without Beethoven's Ninth Symphony, which we intended to have today.'" At the noon meal the conversation is general but "usually sweet little Hephzibah will monopolize it with her beautiful never-ending, always new and delightful French stories, which she reads at her leisure and recites with great delight and original flavor daily."

During the summer, excursions and outdoor life, Yehudi inviting one or another of his favorite playmates, or sometimes all (they are all four years his senior: he is not interested in children his own age).

The press release continues:

During the past year [1928] not less than one hundred offers and invitations have been received, a good many from the most honor-able musical bodies in the world such as the St. Cecilia Academy of Rome, the Philharmonic Orchestras of Berlin, Paris, Stockholm, and Madrid, conservatories and courts of all the continents, not to speak of practically every big city in the United States. Of all these very attractive offers, spontaneously offered, only about a dozen engagements were accepted here and abroad for Yehudi's first tour. Most of the others were indefinitely postponed, but a few have been definitely selected as a nucleus for the 1930 musical season.

Messrs. Evans and Salter, Yehudi's managers, recently an-nounced that after having signed contracts for the carefully selected and limited number of engagements of Yehudi in the principal cities of the East and Middle West (one a week for eight weeks), they had to refuse approximately $200,000 worth of additional offers of engagements for the coming year in accordance with carefully laid plans not to professionalize him too soon.

Most of the engagements accepted are for concerts with an orchestra: less advantageous financially, they are much more enriching from the artistic point of view.

There followed several details on future projects and a list of the works studied in 1928 with Louis Persinger (and new to Yehudi): two concertos by Vivaldi, two by Mozart, two by Vieuxtemps, concertos by Boccherini, Max Bruch, Goldmark, Glazunov, Wieniawski, Sinding, Joachim, the *Kreutzer Sonata* by Beethoven, two Brahms sonatas, the A major and the D minor, a sonata by Nardini, the Vitali Chaconne, the *Clochette, I Palpiti,* and *Streghe* by Paganini, the *Ruralia hungarica* by Kodály, a considerable number of pieces by various authors, the French repertory being represented by Senaillé, Saint-Saëns, Fauré, Pierné, Samazeuilh, and others, and studies by Petri, Ondříček, and Paganini (including the *Perpetual Motion* in fingered octaves!).

Menuhin is now a man. What has been the evolution of his talent? At the risk of vexing certain of his admirers, I should say that toward his fifteenth year, one could detect a certain uneasiness. As a child, his interpretations had a quality of infallibility that made one often imagine that he was the reincarnation of some genius from the past; he also had a tone of such purity that the adjective "celestial" came naturally to the pen of anyone writing about him. Should we credit this to his first teacher, Louis Persinger, which would make him in this respect the greatest pedagogue of all time? At any rate there was a certain period (which coincides with that in which they had the rather singular idea of confiding him to Adolf Busch, who played infinitely less well than he) when his sonority, for a year or two, became stereotyped, his vibrato increased, and some of his interpretations began to lose their beautiful simplicity of line.

He has recovered himself since then. He has found again a style and a sonority of his own. In matters of technique, one could no longer expect from him the infallibilty of a child, ignorant of the possibility of error, or that of a robot-violinist, a champion of speed and endurance. He can, in the same concert, traverse with perfect ease the frightful difficulties of Bartók's Sonata for unaccompanied violin, and miss a sixteenth note in an innocent Mozart allegro. Less constant, more human, his art is perhaps the most seductive synthesis there is of the art of the violin at the present hour. His repertory is enormous, and does not stop growing; he has kept intact his curiosity about all the new music worth reading, but also, outside of his own sphere, of all that can enrich and ripen his personality.

We have recently seen him become passionately interested in the music of the Far East and in the civilizations and forms of thought of which it is an integral part. All this leads one to believe that the radiance of Menuhin far surpasses that of an interpreter, even a gifted one. His activity as a virtuoso is only one of the provinces of a broad humanism, of which there are few equally accomplished examples.

V

Virtuosos

KREISLER

OUR TIME is rich in virtuosos, and there are some
among them whose names have a singular attraction
for the crowds. But I doubt that any can compare
with Fritz Kreisler in his best days.

He was born in Vienna on February 2, 1875. He learned to
read music at the age of three and a half, before he learned the
alphabet. He began by scraping on an instrument made out of
a cigar box strung with shoe laces. At four years he had a toy
violin, and did so well with it that his parents bought him a
real half-size violin.

Accepted at the Vienna Conservatory in 1882, he worked
with Joseph Hellmesberger, Jr., and studied harmony with
Bruckner, who left him with the memory of a musical genius
coexisting with a rather simple spirit. After winning a Gold
Medal for violin at the Vienna Conservatory in 1885, he was
sent to Paris to study under Massart, where two years later he
took the Grand First Prize. In 1888 he made his first tour in
the United States, with Moritz Rosenthal. On his return his
father made him resume his classical studies, which had been
interrupted. He was a student at the Catholic college of the

Piarist friars, then a student of medicine. He gave up medicine, and did his military service in 1895–96. For six years he had practically abandoned the violin. In 1896 he decided to make it his career. He was twenty when he composed his cadenzas for the Beethoven Concerto, cadenzas which won the acclaim of his friend Schoenberg.

After tours in the Orient and in Russia, he made his début with the Vienna Philharmonic under the direction of Hans Richter on January 23, 1898, then in Berlin under the direction of Nikisch, on December 1, 1899.

In 1902 he married Harriet Lies. It was the beginning of a happy married life, and the end of the life of a bachelor whose love of the pleasures of life was in danger of upsetting his equilibrium.

The War of 1914 saw him called up as a lieutenant in the Austrian army. Wounded in the leg and demobilized, he left for the United States, where in spite of some opposition he quickly regained general esteem and admiration. On October 27, 1919, he made a triumphal return at Carnegie Hall. (On October 7, his operetta, *Apple Blossoms*, had obtained a great success at the Globe Theater.) He was applauded again in London in 1921, in Paris in 1924. He resumed his long tours to distant places, but for the first time he had a fixed home, in Berlin-Grünewald (1924).

On December 23, 1933, his second operetta, *Sissy*, was given in Vienna. In May 1938 he was made Commander of the Legion of Honor, and, Austria having passed under the Nazi regime, he obtained French citizenship on May 13, 1939. Soon thereafter, he established himself permanently in New York.

On August 27, 1941, as he was absent-mindedly crossing Madison Avenue, he was run over by a truck and was in a coma for a week. His recovery was far enough advanced in January 1942 so that he made some recordings in the RCA Victor studios.

But the time had come to renounce the concert platform. For his last public appearance, on November 1, 1947, he played the Bach Sonata for solo violin in B minor, Chausson's *Poème*, and the Schumann Fantasy. Subsequently, he was heard only a few times on the air.

My memories of him go far back.

I was a very young man when one fine day I had the privilege of a long conversation with Jacques Thibaud, at the start of his skyrocketing career. I had for him one of those idolatrous admirations which are common in young people (at a distance, it does not seem so unreasonable). As I questioned him avidly about all the things and all the people in his profession, one of his statements struck me, coming from him whom I regarded as the king of violinists. "There is a marvelous fellow," he said, "who will go far beyond me. Remember the name of Kreisler. He is the master of us all."

When Kreisler's first concert was announced, I was at the doors of the hall before the box office was open. I do not think that waiting for a concert to begin ever seemed longer or more exasperating. At last the moment came for his appearance on stage.

Although he was only a little taller than average, Kreisler seemed to me to be a colossus. He gave above all an extraordinary impression of strength, with a large torso, the neck of a shot-putter, a face with strong features topped by a head of thick hair brushed back. Observing him more closely, one saw that the gentleness of his expression softened what at first glance seemed severe.

While the orchestra played the opening tutti he stood as if at attention, arms at his sides, the violin almost touching the ground, with the scroll hooked over the index finger of his left hand. When it was time to start, he indulged in a bit of showmanship by bringing it to his shoulder at the last minute, with a gesture so rapid that the instrument seemed to have been snapped up between his chin and shoulder blade.

Finally we heard him. At this period, the former prize winner at our Conservatory had shaped for himself a technique that would not have found favor with any scholarly jury. He played with very little bow, but with a bow stretched tight enough to break, the stick convex instead of concave as is usual. He succeeded, nevertheless, in holding his notes for an unlimited time, and could soften them to the utmost pianissimo. But this tension on the hair permitted him a bite, a vigor of accent beyond the power of other violinists. When I heard him again after the First World War, he had gone back to more academic principles, to the detriment perhaps of those lightning attacks that literally made his audience jump.

In the cantabile, his tone had a strange seduction, radiant, warm, even sensual, but without any suggestion of coarseness, thanks to the constant firmness of the rhythm which animated all his playing.

Massart's former pupil had inherited from his master an expressive vibrato, very different from that of the German school. He was not afraid to use it to enliven even the passage

work, instead of dividing his playing, as prescribed by the
disciples of Joachim, into vibrant song and passages without
vibrato played with glacial purity. This in no way detracted
from the homogeneity of his style, or from its nobility. In the
great works of the repertory he was the most respectful of
interpreters; he gave free play to his Viennese fantasy in the
little pieces at the end of the concert; and only the mean-
spirited could find anything to censure there, for it was ex-
tremely rare that his personal contribution was not an enrich-
ment. We will see later—but this is another story—that his
imagination sometimes led him beyond a simple cooperation
with the masters of the past.

Kreisler was in reality a composer of merit. While study-
ing violin at the Paris Conservatory, he studied harmony with
Léo Delibes, of whom he evoked for his biographer, Louis P.
Lochner, the happiest memories. Delibes was not a strict task-
master. One day a pretty girl arrived in the midst of a lesson
and took him off dancing. "He would hand me the beginning
of some composition on which he happened to be at work,"
Kreisler recalled, "suggest that I try to catch the spirit of
it, and then charge me with going on from there. Even today
the 'Coppélia' waltz, taken from his ballet, *Coppélia*, is often
played. Well, I can truthfully claim that the motif is mine.
Delibes, returning from one of his adventures with the fair
sex, liked it so well that he took it into his ballet unchanged
and developed and embellished it."

The catalogue of Kreisler compositions attests a perfect
eclecticism. It includes two string quartets, (one from his
early youth has been lost), two operettas, *Apple Blossoms*
and *Sissy*, cadenzas that have become classic for the Beethoven

and Brahms concertos, for four Mozart concertos, and for the Tartini sonata called *The Devil's Trill*, over sixty transcriptions (some of which are obvious concessions to the taste of the least cultivated public), and some forty-five original pieces for the violin.

Among these pieces there are some that have a history, or more exactly, that have had "histories." Beginning around 1905 or 1910, Kreisler often played a certain Concerto in C major by Vivaldi and a dozen shorter pieces which the programs listed as "transcribed from classical manuscripts" of Louis Couperin, Porpora, Pugnani, Padre Martini, et al., as well as three *Old Viennese Dances* sometimes mentioned as the works of Joseph Lanner. These "transcriptions" had an extraordinary success, confirmed by many new printings. For almost half a century there was probably not an amateur violinist who did not play them, or at least massacre them; and professional virtuosos found it expedient, at the end of a recital, to use these short pieces which presented the triple advantage of being admirably written for the instrument, easy to listen to, and signed by names that gave them a high historic dignity.

A reading of the concert reviews for the period of the greatest vogue of these "classical manuscripts" brings to light a touching unanimity of opinion between the critics and the public at large. By a curious twist of fate, it even happened that Kreisler was severely taken to task for having had the "bad taste" to present, alongside this admirable old music, "his own mediocre compositions." And some virtuous Aristarchus fulminated: "After having performed such masterpieces as the *Pavane* and the *Chanson Louis XIII* by Couperin, and Pugnani's *Prelude and Allegro*, how does he dare inflict on us a rendition of his *Caprice viennois*, his *Tambourin chinois*, or his *Liebesleid?*" (Parenthetically, *Liebesleid*—love's sorrow— was one of the three *Old Viennese Dances* published several years previously under Lanner's name.)

I had, personally, reason to be less unsuspecting. The Vivaldi Concerto in C major had made such a strong impression on me that as soon as I heard it I undertook to find the original. It was wasted effort, but I was well compensated, for I gained a deeper acquaintance with the authentic works of the Venetian priest, and acquired the conviction that he could not have been the author of the concerto in question, constructed as it was on a plan brought to its highest point by the contemporaries of Haydn and Mozart.

I had occasion to discover the truth of the matter much later, in the course of a reception given in honor of Kreisler by the singer Ganna Walska (Mrs. McCormick), when he returned to Paris after the First World War. Albert Roussel was there, Honegger also, and Straram, Prunières, Roland-Manuel, André Coeuroy. Kreisler conversed affably with everyone in excellent French, his head not at all turned by the delirious welcome he had just received from the people of Paris. His conversation revealed a sensitive and cultivated man (I shall speak later of his library), as little as possible shut up in his professional world. A little like Thibaud, he was full of anecdotes (alas! the best of them have escaped my memory, after such a long time). I remember only a dialogue with Mischa Elman, who, seeing on his table an *Iliad* in Greek—Kreisler was a good Hellenist and a good Latinist— asked him: "Is that in Hebrew?" "No, Greek." "Is it good?" "Yes, very good." "Does it exist in English?" "Certainly."

"Who is the publisher? . . ."

I took him aside for a minute in a corner of the room to try to clear up the story of the Vivaldi concerto. With a little spark of roguish humor in his eyes, he told me of a monastery somewhere in the South of France, where he had found most of the old manuscripts. I persisted. His smile told me that he knew that I knew; we passed on to other subjects.

Some time later, a violinist more ingenious than scrupulous —we shall call him X . . .—took it into his head to profit from the favor enjoyed by Couperin-Kreisler, Pugnani-Kreisler, etc., and published some Couperin-X . . . , Pugnani-X . . . , which were a simple plagiarism: Kreisler's violin parts copied note for note, with a piano accompaniment unskillfully tacked on.

It was amusing. I recounted this trickery in the second degree in an article on the *Kreisler Transcriptions.* Upon which the real author (for the attributions to Couperin, Pugnani, and others were pure fantasy) turned the tables on X . . . and had the entire infringing edition destroyed.

All this took place around 1925, without causing much excitement. It was another story when, in the beginning of February 1935, Kreisler, answering from Venice an insistent questionnaire from the New York critic Olin Downes, confessed straight out: "The entire series entitled *Classical Manuscripts* is of my composition, except the eight opening measures of the *Chanson Louis XIII* by Louis Couperin, borrowed from a traditional melody. [This is the *Song Composed by the King* (Louis XIII) *and put in tablature by the sieur de La Barre* which Father Mersenne published in 1636 in the section *Des Orgues* of his *Harmonie universelle.*] Necessity inspired

me to this proceeding thirty years ago, when I wished to en-
large my repertory. I felt that to repeat my name constantly on
the program would be awkward and lacking in tact . . ." In
another letter written about the same time, he advanced also
the motive of prudence, which had dissuaded him from sign-
ing his own name and exposing himself to the severe criticism
that virtuoso-composers have every chance of encountering
early in their careers. Such fears were amply justified by his
experience, recounted above, when the *Caprice viennois* and
Tambourin chinois were ridiculed in comparison with the
Classical Manuscripts.

Olin Downes received the confession with a calm smile.
It was not so with his British colleague, Ernest Newman,
who, brusquely abandoning his sense of humor, wrote in
the *Sunday Times* of February 24 a furious article to which
Kreisler made a restrained reply. An answer by Newman. A
new reply by Kreisler, livelier, a little unconsidered, for he
declared: "The names carefully selected were, for the most
part, strictly unknown. Who had ever heard a piece by Pugnani, Cartier, Francoeur, Porpora, Louis Couperin, Padre
Martini, or Stamitz before I began to compose under their
names? They lived exclusively as paragraphs in musical refer-
ence books and their work, when existing and authenticated,
lay mouldering in monasteries and old libraries."

The polemic ended there. Later, Kreisler alluded to it in a
conversation with Louis P. Lochner: "It was a tempest in a
teapot as far as I am concerned. My indignation lasted only
for a few months. I still like to read and reread Newman's
books on Wagner and Mozart, and my respect for him remains
undiminished."

I have somewhat lingered over these "transcriptions" because thanks to the recordings the author made of them, they are the best testimony we have of his gifts as an interpreter.

Listen to the *Prelude and Allegro* formerly attributed to Pugnani, or *Schön Rosmarin* or *Liebesleid*, perfectly executed by one of today's supervirtuosos; then take an old "78" recorded by the composer himself. You will find here a spontaneity, a vivacity, a beauty of tone, a piquancy of accentuation which no one else possesses to the same degree and which give value to the most innocent trifle, to the point where it is difficult to dissociate the work from the interpreter and to appreciate the intrinsic worth of this music. It is not a question of a hierarchy of types, but of the more or less happy inspiration of the moment.

It is certain that Kreisler might have made a large place for himself in light music and rivaled Lehár, Oscar Straus, and others, with infinitely more distinction and harmonic imagination.

I found him one day, during the intermission of a rehearsal, absentmindedly picking out a waltz tune on the piano. I asked him what it was: without being urged, warming up little by little, he played for me almost an act of the operetta, *Sissy*, on which he was then working. His tone on the piano was exquisite. His bouncing rhythm—a rhythm to raise the dead— soon had all the musicians of the orchestra gathered around him.

What struck me more each time, at each new meeting with Kreisler, was the evidence of his musical gift, of a vocation thanks to which music was neither a sport nor a mental exercise nor a game of wit which could be interrupted and resumed, but the vital element to which his whole being was constantly committed.

This gift was revealed in the same way as the boy Mozart's. Kreisler's father was a doctor, a doctor in spite of himself, for he would have been a musician if his family had not opposed it. He consoled himself by playing in a quartet with three other amateurs as music-crazy as he was. The little Fritz listened, all ears. "One day," as he told Lochner, "when I was three and a half years old, I was standing next to my father as he played a Mozart string quartet [Köchel No. 156] with his friends. It started out with the notes, D, B, G. 'How do you know you must play these three notes?' I asked him. Patiently he took a sheet of paper, drew the five lines of a musical staff, and explained what each note meant when written between or on given lines. He also showed how a note was raised or lowered by a half-tone by the use of the sharp and flat signs, and how fractional notes are indicated. I understood at once what he was trying to teach me. And so it came about that I literally could read music before I learned my A, B, C."

At subsequent stages of his musical life, the fortunate boy revealed the same facility. He was admitted to the Vienna Conservatory at the age of seven, where previously no one younger than ten had been accepted. At ten, he took a first prize in violin (the same day he was equally proud that his playmates elected him chief of their band of robbers). Sent to Paris at the age of twelve, in 1887, he took first prize over forty-one contestants.

In his professional preoccupations, technique was secondary. He was never its slave, feeling that if there was a solid base, built in childhood, one could rest on it in all security. He put it this way to a journalist: If a virtuoso has worked hard while he was young, his fingers will always remain supple, so that in his maturity he will not have to tie himself down to a daily regimen to maintain his technique. More precisely he said: "I have hypnotized myself with the thought that I do not need this training, and consequently, I do not need it." According to him, the ripening of talent is better accomplished by reading, ensemble playing, general literary and philosophical culture, than by hours of scales and exercises.

But his appetite for music was inexhaustible. Once in a chamber music session with friends, he asked to play three times over the Schubert quintet for two cellos, which he adored.

For the rest, far from adopting toward the practice of his profession that air of sad resignation which certain of his colleagues affected, he made no secret of the fact that for him this profession was a privileged one. In an interview given to Emile Vuillermoz, he said, "Music has all the characteristics of a vice. It has the violent attraction, the secret pleasures, and the strange detachment. Playing the violin or playing roulette, composing or smoking opium, are tastes that bring their own reward. But musicians are the only people whose 'Vice' is honored and remunerated. When one has virtuosity in the blood, the pleasure of mounting a platform pays one for all his troubles. One would play for nothing. What am I saying? One would pay to play!"

Perhaps it was in gratitude for what he considered such a privilege that Kreisler was always compassionate, and showed a generosity that was legendary among musicians, even though the public at large was little aware of it—for it was discreet. Certain evidences of it were too marked to escape the attention of the press: $26,000, the total receipts of a special concert given on March 27, 1927, at the Metropolitan Opera House, was donated to the American Cancer Society. In January 1949 the $120,372 realized from the sale of his collection of illuminated manuscripts, incunabula, and other treasures, a whole library assembled with love, was divided between two charitable foundations in New York. But those close to Kreisler knew that, at all times, he worked to help his fellow man, materially and morally. When Joseph Szigeti played for the first time in the United States in 1925, he was surprised that he was so quickly taken up by the public and the critics. He learned later that Kreisler had announced to the press that he was the best violinist that Europe had to offer.

Louis P. Lochner recalls that one day, when Kreisler had just landed in an English port, he missed his train and had to wait for the next one. An employee suggested, jokingly, that he kill time by giving a little recital. In the cold, dingy atmosphere of the station, Kreisler took out his violin, played for the customs officials, railwaymen, and dockers, and when he had finished his concert, gently expressed the hope that they had enjoyed it!

At the end of the First World War he took under his wing forty-three orphans left by his fellow soldiers. When he was living in Berlin, he invited sixty little waifs for Christmas. Eighty-five came. "My party is going well," he said, happily rubbing his hands together.

After the last war, he sent food packages in profusion to Europe. Someone observed that many of these packages were stolen before reaching their destination. To which his wife, who completely shared his way of looking at things, replied calmly, "And what of it? It is always eaten by someone. Even a dishonest mailman has a family to feed."

He never began a concert tour in France without giving the proceeds of the first concert to a charity.

The program of a recital he gave at the Opéra on November 15, 1924, carried this dedication:

"With the compliments of M. Fritz Kreisler for his old friends of the Paris Conservatory and for the Soldiers Blinded in the War." Each copy bore his autograph.

I could report a hundred such incidents. I shall tell only one more, because it touches me closely. In April 1946, an association that had been formed to assist artists and intellectuals uprooted by the war was trying to buttress its tottering treasury. I had the idea of asking Kreisler if he would be willing, should he come to Europe, to reserve for this association part of the benefits of his first concert, according to his custom.

I received by return mail, I, who was not a friend but only an admirer of long standing, a letter in which there was no question of a projected tour, but which contained a check for 50,000 francs, with almost an apology.

"I regret infinitely that the reduction of my current means because of world events and a large number of other demands (sometimes prickly but always unavoidable) prevent me from sending more.

With my warmest friendly greetings,
Always your devoted F.K."

Jarnowick
(AN ENGRAVING BY L. SCOTTI, C. 1790)

*Announcement of the first
performance of
Beethoven's Concerto*

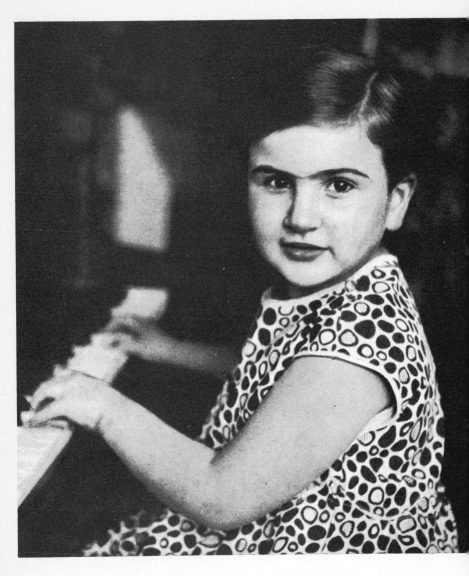

Ruth Slenczynski at the age of seven
(PARIS, 1932)

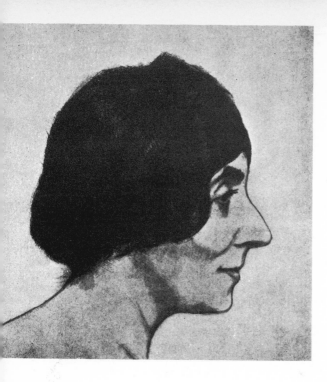

Wanda Landowska
in 1917

Alexandre Boucher
AN ANONYMOUS LITHOGRAPH, BERLIN, 1821

THE MODERN ORPHEUS.

Opera House – June 5ᵈ 1831.

Sketches of the Musical World Nᵒ 1 to be continued

London Published by Thoˢ Mᶜ Lean, June 10ᵗʰ 1831, 26 Haymarket

Printed by C Hullmandel 51 St Martins Lane.

Paganini in London in 1831

ce 6 Marce 1791

Machere fille je cre que tre teriblemen
ocupe a tonclasecen puisque jenn silontan
sanrerevoer de letre detoe — cela neman
pechie pa de t'ecrire purtaprandre tut
cequime tarive netatanpar adebone nuvele
car jenane que demouere a taprandre
anarivant adublen le docter clarque — jema
~~tande~~ evenu menaer je matande aloer
unome duncertenaje — paendutu jeue un
jenome danviron 24 ana — quire docter demusique
sanranduter — paria protecsion — du vicerol
quimancepa danantaje — g jur avan le premie
concer — jeue dantepapie qu'iletanonce su
ladirecsion dudocter clarque — de M^e ienevic
etan forsurmi je fiu chieledocter — eluidi
que moncontra e tez suladirecsion dudocter
clarque e non su la direcsion de M^e ienevic
il more pondu qu'iletet arosie avec jenevic
pour partajer le risque delantreprire — je
luie repondu qu'un ienevic netet didune
fortune a merepondre de monar jan ni
dune reputasion a etre mon directer — e
que jenejurepa — susadirecsion = Eucome
a malitre reçu pour ça avoir situare susarjan

Jarnowick's letter to his daughter dated March 6, 1791

Paris le 16 Juin 1838

Monsieur

Je suis forcé de vous exprimer ma surprise en voyant le peu de fourceur que vous mettez à remplir la dette que vous avez envers moi. — Cette négligence de votre part m'obligera de vous rafraîchir la mémoire sur des circonstances que vous ne devez pas avoir oubliées.

Je vous présente donc mon petit compte en vous priant de vouloir bien le solder au plutôt. —

Pour avoir donné douze leçons à Mademoiselle votre fille afin de lui faire comprendre la manière dont elle devait — exprimer la musique, et le sens des notes qu'elle exécutait en ma présence. 2,400 francs. —

Pour avoir moi même exécuté chez vous pendant huit fois en différentes occasions: plusieurs morceaux de musique. — 24,000 francs.

Total 26,400 francs —

Je n'ajoute point à ce compte tous les leçons que j'ai donné verbalement à Mademoiselle votre fille, pendant que j'étais à votre table, tout en payant ma part jusqu'au dernier centime, voulant bien lui faire un cadeau des pièces que je suis prêté dans ces moments, pour tâcher de lui donner les véritables idées de la science musicale, désirant qu'elle ait pu les saisir, et en profiter.

Je n'ajouterai point non plus, aucun mot pour vous faire connaître qu'il est juste de payer les personnes qui nous rendent des services et nous prêtent des soins, puisque

vous n'avez pas manqué, de me dire sur ce point votre
opinion en me donnant des avis dur l'affaire du Docteur
Cr.....o par lesquels vous avez jugé à propos que je dusse
payer cent dix fr pour n'avoir reçu, heureusement pour
ma santé, que quelques conseils qui ne me furent donnés que
par hazard chez vous. Vous dictez bien, Monsieur, qu'il passe
une trop grande différence entre les soit-disantes visites de
ce Docteur à mes Leçons, et plus encore à mes séances
d'exécution pour ne pas connoître, qu'en proportion,
je suis bien plus modeste dans mes demandes, qu'il ne
l'est dans les siennes. .

    Je vous prie donc, de vous acquitter, de suite de la dette
que vous avez envers moi, car je vous préviens qu'en cas
contraire, je ne manquerai pas certainement, de suivre
l'exemple que les autres me donnent, étant bien persuadé,
d'en avoir, au moins, le même droit.

    Je vous salue bien distinctement, et j'ai l'honneur d'être

Nicolò Paganini

Monsieur Loveday

copié Monsieur
Monsieur Loveday
Rue St Lazare 40
Paris

La lettre dont la copie est ci dessus,
existe chez M. Loveday, N° 40
Rue St Lazare en attendant qu'elle
soit déposée au Musée ou dans
les Archives des hommes extraordinaires

Loveday

uglas Loveday

Alexandre Boucher's letter to Giacomelli

I believe that this goodness and simplicity were not only dominant traits in Kreisler's character; they certainly marked in large part his genius as an interpreter. However accomplished his technique, violinists of the younger generation have equalled it, perhaps surpassed it. He was the first to say so. In the conversation with Emile Vuillermoz to which I referred above, he declared: "The professional level of young violinists today sincerely astounds me. There are at this moment hundreds of young students who have, I do not say the genius, but the professional equipment of Paganini. No technical difficulty impedes them. They are capable of playing with ease all that is most difficult in the literature of their instrument, and this is a novelty in the history of instrumental music. But from the standpoint of genius of interpretation and of that mysterious force which is the radioactivity of a great performer, our century is not very different from the others."

In fact, Kreisler's prowess as a virtuoso seems to be within reach of numerous contemporary violinists. But they will find it difficult to match his generosity, his persuasive charm, the human accent of his playing, which combined in an ideal way a Latin clarity and a certain Viennese sentimentality, inherited from Romanticism, whose chances of surviving, now that Alban Berg is no longer with us, are fragile indeed.

WANDA LANDOWSKA
and the
REVIVAL of the HARPSICHORD

The history of the harpsichord unfolds in two periods curiously separated by an interval of more than a century.

The first extends from the beginning of the fifteenth century to the last third of the eighteenth. The second began about 1900, with the first concerts of Wanda Landowska.

It is not literally exact that we owe to Landowska the idea of undertaking the construction of harpsichords in the contemporary era. A good number of errors have also been put into circulation concerning her beginnings. She allowed some of them to gain credence, either for the pleasure of mystification (one of the oriental sides of a very complex personality), or through a coquetry that was the only weakness of that pure spirit.

Thus on the date of her birth: musical dictionaries published before 1926 (Eaglefield Hull, Riemann) had her born in Warsaw on July 5, 1877; Grove's dictionary, in 1927, gives July 5, 1880; the French Riemann of 1931 gives July 5, 1884. Now it is certain that when she came to France in 1900, neither her physical appearance nor her artistic maturity was that of an adolescent of sixteen summers. It is also said that at that time she inspired the firm of Pleyel to make a modern harpsichord, and this is neither entirely true nor entirely false. She arrived in Paris already an accomplished pianist. Now just at that moment a little group of musicians and musicologists (whom I knew well soon thereafter) had joined together to revive the repertory of the seventeenth and eighteenth centuries. Laloy, Prod'homme, de La Laurencie, Pirro, Quittard, and more than anyone, Ecorcheville, the founder of the journal *S.I.M.* (the organ of the French section of the International Society of Music), were waiting for the harpsichordist who would bring to life the instrument constructed more than ten years previously from the plans of Gustave

Lyon, head of the house of Pleyel. For the modern harpsichord existed: one was shown at the World's Fair of 1889,
and Louis Diémer had played it in public at a Couperin recital
on December 9, 1891; but his undeniable virtuosity was not
enough to bring back to life the music he had exhumed. It fell
to Wanda Landowska to bring this music from the realm of
archeology to that of reality, to give those shadowy works
by Purcell, Couperin, and Rameau the breath of life, the
animation, the persuasive force by which the Classicists, the
Romanticists, and their successors have enthralled us. Certainly
it is to Wanda's initiative and persistence that we owe the
addition to the harpsichord of the low stop, called the "16-foot
stop," which Gustave Lyon achieved in 1912. But she had
not waited until then to take up her crusade. Hardly had she
begun to perform in public as a clavecinist than one had the
feeling of being present at the veritable resurrection of a forgotten art, whose prodigious richness no one had suspected:
her dazzling demonstration of its real existence was a far cry
from the theoretical knowledge held by that little circle of
musicologists I mentioned earlier.

I find evidence of how impressive this demonstration was
in a report addressed from London to the German Bulletin
of the International Society of Music. Reviewing a concert
of Wanda's at the Queen's Hall, the English critic declared:
"There was such a palpitation of life in her interpretations
that if Bach and Couperin had appeared on the platform to
acknowledge the applause, it would have seemed perfectly
natural."

But the intrepid virtuoso did not limit herself to the role
of performer alone. She wished not only to seduce, but to

convince, which could not come about without a persevering struggle against all sorts of opposition. The most violent was that of the pianists who saw a part of their repertory menaced if it were proved that the new instrument was more adept than theirs in translating the sonatas of Scarlatti, the fugues of the *Well-Tempered Clavier*, and the several concert encores borrowed from Couperin, Daquin, and Rameau. "I have remarked in the course of my travels," wrote Wanda, (*S.I.M.*, May 1910) "that the harpsichord met its antagonists principally among the pianists. The trouble of procuring an instrument that is difficult to handle and of acquiring a special technique is not the only motive for this mistrust. There are deeper and more serious reasons. When one has been accustomed since childhood to hear certain works on the piano, it is rather natural that one should experience a certain shock at first when the same pieces are played with absolutely different sonorities. Our ears are at first too surprised by these silvery timbres, these metallic chords, too dazzled by this luminous éclat and this mysterious humming to be able to follow the melodic idea and to feel its expression."

Fortified by a musicological erudition which became more and more solid, she reinforced her polemics with citations taken from the original sources, all the more efficacious because they were presented with a radiant good humor, just the thing to disarm learned men with long beards. A professor from beyond the Rhine insisted at all costs that J. S. Bach would have preferred the clavichord to the harpsichord, the former an instrument which possesses neither the same power, nor the same timbre, nor the same polyphonic possibilities. (This error goes back to the most respectable savants, Spitta foremost, and Wanda gives the reasons.) She replies:

"There is an old story, very popular in the eighteenth century, of a soldier, who, passing through a forest, sat down under a tree to take some nourishment. He took some bread and cheese from his knapsack, but he had hardly begun to eat when he saw two wolves whose famished look warned him that they wanted to join the feast. To keep them from coming too near, he threw them several pieces, until everything was eaten. Not knowing what to do next to escape them, he took it into his head to play his bagpipe, and hardly had he begun when the terrified wolves took flight. . . .

"If the little wolves who want to destroy my harpsichord are not satisfied with the morsels I throw them, I know some tunes on the bagpipe that will make them run away forever. . . . They are Bach's authentic titles." With great effect, she lists a series of titles taken either from autograph manuscripts or from collections engraved during the life of J. S. Bach, in which the use of the harpsichord is specified without the least ambiguity.

In the same jovial tone, but one which makes its point as surely as a solemn argument, she makes a case against those pseudo-traditions that destroy all that gave life and lustre to the old music:

"They tell the story where I come from of a peasant who said to his wife:

" 'You know, up there, at the castle, they are crazy about cherry tarts. You ought to make one someday.'—'But butter is dear.'—'Make it without butter.'—'And the eggs?'—'We can do without eggs.'—'And then, you know, the cherry season is over.'—'Oh, make it without cherries, it doesn't matter.'

"The peasant tastes the tart and cries:

'Rich people must be stupid to go crazy over something that has no taste!' "

Those are some fragmentary traits, the easiest to capture, of a many-sided personality, impossible to enclose in a definition. No one has let us see its richness better than André Schaeffner, in a study whose concluding paragraph I quote:

Her interpretation, all intelligence and sensuality mingled, cannot be conceived apart from the reasoning and practical spirit and the oriental imagination which are met thus in a single body. This sense of action of which we spoke, the moments when all softness, all caress abandoned, Wanda Landowska shows herself as the flaming torch which she could be; this near-deviltry (of which she is not always conscious) such as the Hoffmannesque apparition, in the piece by Rameau, of a ghost-like third hand, surging from below a system of lines so firm, so resolved, so logically deduced; her "look of a sleeper awakened" and her "siren" charms, which Maurras noted in George Sand; those moments of vertigo which made her the bacchante of the old music, when, in the intimacy of her studio, we saw a thin face with prominent cheekbones, the whole person gaunt, neither beautiful nor ugly—ageless, with a physical strength as if borrowed from the elements and as irresponsible as they, manipulating a harpsichord as big as an organ; all this was inimitable, and leads one to think that music made in this manner is more truly music than that gathering dust on library shelves or heard in stuffy concerts. (*Revue Musicale*, June 1927.)

This transfiguration by music, this second state in which the interpreter seems to relive each of the masters he evokes, is the privilege of certain chosen artists. Landowska had it in the highest degree. In order to achieve it, she did not need the stimulus of a large audience. Often, but especially in the years after the First World War, I had the privilege of being the only listener in the quiet of her salon-studio on the Rue Lapeyrère.

I had made her acquaintance soon after her return to Paris in 1920 (the war had surprised her in Berlin, where she taught harpsichord at the Hochschule, and she had to stay there until after the Armistice).

When they dispersed the fine library of Ecorcheville, who was killed in battle early in 1915, I sat beside Wanda during the four evenings of the sale. We had more than one reason to be friendly: the same sad memory of the dead man, to whom we both owed a debt of gratitude (he had guided my start as a musicologist with unforgettable kindness), many common ideas and curiosities about all that concerned our art, and, as for the immediate moment, we coveted almost the same works, without too much bitterness, withdrawing in turn in each other's favor.

From that time on there dated a friendship which never flagged, but which was particularly enriching during the period which preceded her installation at Saint-Leu—we lived very near each other. I still have some notes of hers in which she asked me for a book or some information. They would be the occasion for a visit that could last for hours, for the conversation would invariably lead her to sit down at the harpsichord or the piano. Those who did not hear her in the intimacy of her home can form only an incomplete idea of her genius as an interpretive artist and an improviser. As a pianist,

she never appeared in public except in the sonatas and concertos of Mozart. But she played Schubert, Chopin, and the
other Romantics marvelously. I never heard from other hands
the same rhythmic surge, the freedom of modulation, the
exquisite freshness of Schubert's *Ländler*.

I have been rereading letters of hers which I saved, written
in a lively style, full of images, as was her conversation. I
remember her triumphs, in the years 1922 to 1925, at the Concerts Koussevitzky, and those concerts, more impressive still,
which she gave with the singer Maria Barrientos, with the flutist
Louis Fleury, or those which made a veritable temple of
music of the hall she built in her garden at Saint-Leu, and
which she inaugurated on July 3, 1927. But it would take a
volume to evoke the heroic times of the resurrection of the
harpsichord. I shall merely recall that under the influence of
Wanda Landowska, and under her influence alone, Manuel
de Falla, from 1923 on, introduced the harpsichord into the
orchestration of the *Retablo de Maese Pedro*, and in 1926
wrote his Concerto for harpsichord, which preceded by one
year the *Concert champêtre* by Poulenc. The spark had been
struck. Since then, Stravinsky, Florent Schmitt, Roland-
Manuel, and Frank Martin among others, have used the harpsichord, alone or with various combinations of instruments.
From the school of Saint-Leu have come world-famous clav-
ecinists, who in turn have their own followers: Ruggero
Gerlin, Isabelle Nef, Aimée Van de Wiele, and others. . . .

All this is the work of Wanda Landowska. What does it
matter, then, that she was not the first to have the idea of
reconstructing harpsichords? Before Landowska, the recon-
structions had mainly an archeological interest; they were

museum pieces, without a soul and without a future. It was she who gave them a new life, assuring not only the resurrection of the masterpieces of past centuries, but the flowering of a new "art of playing the harpsichord."

GEORGES ENESCO

I still see, a long time later, the poster announcing the coming of Enesco to the city in western France where I was finishing my studies. I remember my enthusiasm mixed with an intense curiosity.

He was to play the Beethoven Concerto, some fragments from a Bach Suite for solo violin, and to direct his two *Rumanian Rhapsodies*. So many fascinating enigmas! In the hands of mediocre interpreters, the Beethoven Concerto had up to then seemed to me long, dry, and boring: what was it really like? After the full orchestra, how would the frail strings of the violin sound in the Bach? What could be expected of the *Rumanian Rhapsodies*, written some ten years previously by a composer just out of the cradle?

Enesco's personality had already spread beyond the coteries. Although he was admired and adulated, one knew that he also had detractors. Some good judges called him a genius; a few violinists refused to credit him with any talent.

The echoes of the first rehearsal promptly discredited the latter. The orchestra was conquered, and its members spread throughout the city an acclaim which mounted from hour to hour. Perhaps it was as a conductor that he most astonished the musicians. He revealed them to themselves, drawing an unsuspected amplitude and precision from an ensemble full of good will but ordinarily timid in its enthusiasm. In a few minutes, with the skill of a veteran, he had succeeded in shaping even those passages reputed to be unplayable. And even in the Concerto, where the tremendous solo absorbed him, his playing possessed a quality of eloquence which raised his partners almost to his level of excitement.

His technique as a violinist, they said, was absolutely original. Scorning academic principles, he held his right arm away from the body, the elbow raised, the wrist overhanging the violin; and he used a loosely strung bow from which he nevertheless obtained a tone that carried to the farthest reaches of the hall. The strength of the fingers of his left hand was such that in the bravura passages one heard the percussion of each note; he had a dry, almost electric trill. No other tone resembled his, warm, expressive, with sometimes a slight hoarseness in the background, something sad and singularly moving.

Thus the orchestra commented on its hero. One of the women musicians aroused jealousies by gathering up the pieces of an E string broken in full action, and distributing the tiny fragments parsimoniously to a few privileged friends.

Came the concert. The hall overheated, an atmosphere of anxious waiting. The tuning-up of the orchestra could only increase the general impatience.

At length he arrives: tall, his pale face framed with long hair, his expression distant. The Concerto begins, the timpani mark the rhythm of the interminable tutti, which all the same reaches its peroration.

Enesco starts to play, and the promised charm operates from the first measures: he scales the chain of octaves at the beginning with that henceforth unforgettable tone, a mélange, impossible to analyze, of intellectuality and sensual emotion, with a noble amplitude, and especially with that musical eloquence, the gift above all others which resists analysis, which gives to each melodic line a sense and a form, and transforms into living phrases the passage work, which can be dull sequences of notes under the fingers of those in whom inspiration does not dwell.

The audience saw some rare minutes. A common fervor united the separate individuals. Even those most impervious to music followed without wearying the wandering arabesque that the violin unfolded above the great voice of the orchestra. Joachim's long cadenza, hopeless under the academic bow of a Beethoven specialist, here took on a symphonic sense, so that interest, instead of lagging, mounted to a climax. On a long trill, progressively quieter, the theme re-entered, one of the simplest and most beautiful that man has ever invented. The solo instrument, which up to then had only given us glimpses of it, surrounding it from a distance with delicate embroidery, expressed it here for the first and only time in its poignant nudity. With a sort of religious precaution, Enesco approached it so softly, so tenderly, that hearts were melted, breathing was suspended, and, when the last chord had been struck, a total silence reigned for several seconds before a tremendous applause rolled across the theater. People wept with emotion.

As blasé as I may be, after a long experience of concertgoing, I do not feel, from this distance, any astonishment. It is because in addition to the prestige exercised by great technique and eloquence of interpretation, one of the singular attributes of virtuosity was revealed to us all. I speak of that mysterious influence which for want of a better name we call magnetism. It seems to radiate from the soloist; it invests him, for a time, with a sovereign authority over a subdued orchestra, over a public "charmed" in the magic sense of the word, so completely that no critical spirit can daunt it, as long as the spell lasts.

But do not hasten to rejoice for the virtuoso. Such a privilege has its troublesome counterpart. The illumination of the first triumph is so violent that it fixes in the memory of the hearer a certain indelible image to which the virtuoso is expected to conform for the rest of his life.

And if he should be restive, too bad for him. And if he should decide to be something other than a virtuoso, too bad; all-engrossing virtuosity puts a wall around him. For most of their contemporaries, Frescobaldi, Corelli, Couperin merited admiration above all for their skill as an organist, a violinist, a harpsichordist. The composer of *Les Préludes*, of *Mazeppa*, of *Christus* was hidden until after his death by the Liszt of the *Hungarian Rhapsodies*.

A similar injustice has taken place under our eyes in regard to Enesco. His career as a performer developed splendidly after that early revelation in the Concerto in D. His interpretations of Bach and of Beethoven were authoritative. If Mozart suited him less well—even in deepest sorrow the divine master of Salzburg keeps a transparency of style that was not Enesco's forte—he entered oftener than anyone else into the thought of Schumann, of Brahms, of the Fauré of the second Sonata, whose interior drama he alone seemed to be able to penetrate.

A spell-binding violinist, in whom the well-informed, around the year 2000, will be taking credit for discovering

one of the most remarkable composers of our time. Outside
of professional circles it is known more or less vaguely that he
wrote some noble music, but it seems that the performer
monopolized all the faculties of attention and admiration that
the general public of his time was capable of. The person most
concerned manifested no anxiety, as if he left to an immanent
justice the duty of eventually revising its values.

However, composing was not for him the pastime or the
consolation of a jaded virtuoso. More than one, in effect, after
his career is over, has taken with a pretty zeal to blackening
the staves, without suspecting that he is producing nothing of
which he has not heard a forerunner, and which a more or
less extended reworking in the depths of his subconscious has
not succeeded in making new.

With Enesco, the gift of creating music went back to his
early youth, to the tender age when he scratched the first
notes on the toy violin brought at his entreaty from the
neighboring city. Even then he tried to set down his im-
provisations, having never opened a book of theory, rein-
venting for his own use the elements of the art. His stay at the
Vienna Conservatory gave him a foundation which allowed
him to write, at the age of fourteen, a quintet for piano and
strings which was far from being the work of a schoolboy.
Hugues Imbert, who heard it in 1897 at an intimate recital,
has told of his surprise in the presence of a work already so
well-balanced and above all of such a striking originality, in
spite of turns of phrase which revealed a convinced follower
of Brahms. Enesco's real début as a composer dates from the
following year, when he was still a student at the Paris Conservatory. On February 3, 1898, at the Châtelet, Edouard

Colonne directed the first performance of the *Poème roumain*, Opus 1. It is a sort of *Pastoral Symphony* in which the author retraces his childhood impressions. In spite of some naïveté, an occasionally academic style, and a rather tinselly dramatic sentiment, there is nevertheless a valuable affirmation of personality and boldness. This adolescent is not afraid to think big! One hundred forty pages of score in closely-written text, and a score which rings with variety as well as brilliance. His gifts as an orchestrator will be more manifest still in the two *Rumanian Rhapsodies*, composed soon after and inspired also by the national folklore. More concise, unblemished by any "development for development's sake," they have lost through the years none of their rustic freshness and vivacity of style.

Next come some pieces for the piano. Here one cannot help being astonished at the indifference of concert artists. If the Suite in the old style (Opus 3) is in some ways a pastiche, the second Suite, with titles no less archaistic—Toccata, Sarabande, Pavane, Bourrée—abounds in invention. Enesco's astounding ability as a pianist (those who heard him play from memory the *Prelude to the Afternoon of a Faun* or entire episodes from the *Rite of Spring* will not find that adjective exaggerated) brought to him, the composer, a knowledge, or better yet, a subtle intuition of the resources of the keyboard and the pedals. Treated orchestrally, this counterpoint comes alive, illuminates the apparent complications of the writing, which are revealed as necessary and lovely. We willingly admit that this technique of execution is not within the powers of the first one to come along. One can never emphasize enough how Enesco was haunted by a concern for tonal color.

Even when playing a piece for solo violin, he never ceased to combine or oppose different timbres. Thanks to this he was perhaps the only violinist under whose bow the fugues of Bach held the listener spellbound to the end.

Around 1900, an important transformation takes place. The refinements of writing give way to a concern for expression. This is the period of romantic exaltation in which the first two sonatas for piano and violin are written. The first is very uneven, hampered by the desire for a classical orthodoxy ill-attuned to the character of the ideas; the second realizes a perfect accord of form and material, with its ardent lyricism, its tormented writing which greatly surprised the audience when it was given in 1899 at one of the little Thursday Concerts Colonne. Here the young master evolved with deceptive rapidity toward a more complex form, a harmonic system completely different from that which was esteemed in the works of Massenet, Saint-Saëns, Lalo. One became aware, after a close analysis, of the boldness of his musical language, at a time when boldness was far from assuring success. The late Jean Huré commented with insight on Enesco's role as a precursor, after the failure of the *Symphonie concertante* in 1908:

"It must be said aloud, Enesco is one of those who impose musical forms and not one of those who submit to them . . . His talent is absolutely sure and if it sometimes seems disconcerting to us, it is because a superior genius puts him above our comprehension.

"It would be naive to judge Enesco by the same criteria that we apply so easily to other contemporaries . . . Georges Enesco is the most 'modern' of contemporary composers. It seems as if the delightful author of *Pelléas* was twenty-five years behind the musician of the *Dixtet*."

The Octet, presented by the Geloso and Chailley quartets at the Thursday Concerts Colonne, shocked the public even more. Colonne himself proved refractory. To one of his friends who exclaimed "It is terribly beautiful!" he replied in a cutting tone: "How right that is! But it is more terrible than beautiful!" The audience itself deliberately refused to accept the tension of a development that was rich perhaps to excess, and especially the bitter and willful character of a harmony for which the suavities of growing Impressionism had scarcely prepared it. And the Octet was withdrawn from the programs.

Far from joining the Debussy bandwagon, as so many others did, Enesco was thrown back toward the Wagner of the *Meistersinger*, toward an ever richer polyphony, that of his Symphony in E-flat (first heard on January 21, 1906), that of his *Symphonie concertante*, of his Suite for Orchestra Opus 9, of the quartet with piano, of the *Dixtet* for wind instruments. The *Chansons of Clément Marot*, limpid and without surcharge, alone escape this tendency.

Enesco told me one day how the Wagnerian spell was rudely broken by the First World War (which otherwise was to lead—the remark is not his—so many new listeners to the master of *Tristan*, aided by the excesses of the anti-Wagnerians!).

He was mobilized on the spot, in Rumania, and detailed to service with the wounded. Bending over their wounds, seeing at close quarters these soldiers from his native land, these stoic peasants, hardened to pain, resigned to death if that was their destiny, he was filled with admiration and boundless gratitude.

His deepest being, his sensibility as a musician, was transformed. In his previous existence as a wandering virtuoso, feted in all the capitals, a guest in drawing-rooms almost indistinguishable one from another, whether in Paris, Vienna, or St. Petersburg, he had thought himself a citizen of the world. Now his atavism returned. When the whirlwind had passed and he set himself to compose again, his works were impregnated by Rumanian folk-music, without textual borrowing, without any stock "effects" of shoddy orientalism. The change was more profound: an art of Western refinement was re-immersed, in the East, in a bath of youth and freshness, and drew from it new strength, a flowering of ideas and rhythms.

Such was the impression created by his String Quartet (first played by the Flonzaley Quartet), by his Third Symphony (1921), and especially by the *Oedipus*, from which Enesco directed three *Dances* at the Concerts Colonne in March 1924, this time obtaining a triumphal success.

These notes have, I hope, some value, now that Georges Enesco is dead. He died on May 4, 1955. The younger generation will probably not realize what his going means. For some years Enesco had performed as a violinist only with reluctance. The illness that weakened him made his playing more and more uneven; he was conscious of this, and feeling his strength ebbing each day, he found it more and more intolerable to take the least bit of time from what was his reason for living: writing music. I remember with what vivacity he told me this at one of our last meetings, some years ago in Siena. Every afternoon at five o'clock he gave a course at Count Chigi's Academy. He was then so weak that he had to rest in bed until the hour for the course. He received me in his bedroom; the conversation followed the normal course until I had the foolish idea of asking him: "Do you still compose?" His eyes lit up as if I had said something offensive. "More than ever!" he shot out, crossly. But almost at once he smiled at his impulsiveness, and carefully explained to me what he had recently told Bernard Gavoty and had told other interviewers long ago, but in the form of sallies I had only half-believed: he hated his activity as a virtuoso, he regarded the violin as his worst enemy, obliged as he was to devote to it some time stolen from his passion, his mission as a composer. He was above all else a polyphonist, he needed the many voices of the orchestra, beside which the solo instrument seemed thin and unsatisfying. And I agreed, thinking of his symphonies, of his great opera, *Oedipus*, whose revival was so long delayed.

But at the same time I saw again in my mind's eye the virtuoso he had been in his radiant youth. Behind this graying man, exhausted, emaciated as an El Greco, who lived only by the expression of his eyes, arose the image of Enesco as he had appeared to me for the first time, almost half a century ago.

I had just heard him spoken of, by chance, in the most disparaging way. Rejoining the provincial school where I was a boarding student, I found myself on the same train with the musicians of the orchestra of Angers, who greatly impressed me with their peremptory judgments on the celebrities of the moment. One of them having named Georges Enesco, there was unleashed a fine chain of slanders: he had no talent, he was an *arriviste* taken up by snobs. . . . Then soon afterwards the concert of which I spoke above took place. I shall not return to it, except to repeat the impression of genius that

was irresistibly given to everyone by this tall thin boy with
the fine pensive face, of whom it appeared that music was the
natural element, the life-giving milieu. No other musician has
made me feel this to a similar degree, and I experienced it again
each time I saw him. His memory had stored away the music
of all periods and all schools. When shortly before his death
he accompanied Marcelle Bunlet, playing a whole act of
Götterdämmerung from memory, he made an orchestra out
of the piano.

But this immense knowledge did not affect his personality
as a composer, as his teacher André Gedalge bore witness in
a letter written in 1923, when, speaking of his recent pupils,
he concluded: "The only one of them all, to my mind, who
has a real personality and who does not give the impression
that he deforms current ideas to make them appear new,
is Enesco. At bottom, and this is my whole thought, he is the
only one to have real ideas and inspiration."

I cannot hope to have given in these few pages the measure
of an artist who was great among the great, and who added
to his creative gifts an immense generosity, a boundless sympathy of which a thousand examples could be told. I merely
add to all the homages which are and will be tendered him
that of an admiration which has never flagged.

VI

Eccentric Virtuosos

THE ILLITERATE JARNOVICK

FICTIONALIZED biographies are all the rage. There is such a frightful consumption of great men on the part of the publishers that one can foresee that the supply will soon be exhausted. At this moment, when the curiosity of the public must be satisfied willy nilly with heroes of the second degree, here is a strange virtuoso, whose ringing name and adventurous life, full of sudden turns of fate, of contrasts and mysteries, will attract the author in search of a personality: Giovanni Mane Giornovichi, called Jarnovick.

At the present time he is unknown. The biographical dictionaries repeat under his name a handful of anecdotes and few precise facts (one must go to some trouble to collect them)—as if it were not a question here of the violinist who for twenty years was the most famous in Europe, the most idolized, and probably the best.

Certain biographers, among them Arteaga, the well-informed author of the *Révolutions du théâtre musical italien*, have him born in Paris in 1745. According to Fétis, he indicated in his own hand in 1784, in the register of the great Masonic Lodge of Berlin, that he came from Palermo; and the Czech composer Gyrowetz, his contemporary, who had ties of friendship with him, declares in his *Memoirs* that he was born in a boat in the territorial waters of Ragusa (now Dubrovnik) and so found himself a man without a country.

But we know with certainty that, according to the sacred formula, he "showed from infancy a very evident disposition for music," and that he studied the violin with Lolli, a prodigious performer, a little crack-brained, a worthy teacher of a worthy pupil. There is no other information on his youth until around his twentieth year. In 1767 he was installed in Paris in the Rue St. Lazare as a teacher of the violin.

Here the novelist-biographer can imagine a plausible link of consanguinity with a certain Gernovichi, who in April 1761 had opened on the boulevards a shop dealing in Venetian marionettes.

Glory came to him suddenly. At the Concert Spirituel of March 25, 1773, after having played Lolli's sixth concerto without great success, Jarnovick aroused enthusiasm with one of his own works, his First Concerto, in A major. Not only did he triumph, but his style became the model that everyone tried to copy. The most famous of his rivals tried vainly to compete against his new fame. In Easter week of 1775, La Motte himself, the king of staccato, barely succeeded "in holding his own in the votes of the cognoscenti" in the first round, if it can be called that; in the second, which took place a few days later, on Low Sunday, the victory went to Jarnovick, whose purity of tone, precision, and charm won out incontestably. His name appears often in subsequent programs of the Concert Spirituel, where his concertos are often performed by others. Sometimes, with Le Duc, Le Brun, Duport, he plays little airs arranged for quartet in the manner of the time. He is sought after in the drawing-rooms. He makes music at the salon of Mme. de Genlis, at the home of Baron de Bagge with his pupil Pieltain (we shall see later to what a point master and pupil pushed their rivalry one fine day). The *Mémoires secrets* (by the successors of Bachaumont) mention a concert given for his benefit in March 1777 in a room lent by the Prince de Guémenée, and remark that at the Concert Spirituel at which Jarnovick performed at the end of the same month in the presence of Queen Marie Antoinette, she visibly refrained from applauding. Doubtless he had committed one of those breaches of etiquette which were customary with him.

Suddenly, in 1779, for reasons which remain obscure, he left France. King Frederick William II of Prussia engaged him; at the end of four years his misunderstanding with the other artists of the orchestra, in particular with Duport, was beyond repair. He left Prussia and traveled back and forth across the continent, as mobile as if he were living in the age of the railroad and the airplane. He was applauded in Switzerland, in Germany, in Austria (it was in Vienna that he came to know Gyrowetz, at the salon of a patron of music, Franz Bernhard von Kees, where he also met Haydn, Mozart, and Dittersdorf), in Poland, in Scandinavia, in Russia. The vogue for his music did not seem to decline in France for all that. In 1781 alone, his concertos appeared half a dozen times on the programs of the Concert Spirituel. In 1790, anticipating the recent innovation of our national theaters, the choreographer Gardel had the second act of his ballet, *Télémaque*, danced to a concerto by Jarnovick, with only a partial success. "The idea," observed the critic of the *Gazette nationale*, "is not perhaps a

happy one. Our attention cannot be divided equally. Those
who are more sensitive to the dance than to music (and this is
the greater number) missed all the merit of the concerto,
which was, however, perfectly performed." In 1791 Jarnovick
arrived in London, went from there to Ireland and Scotland,
returned to London, made himself insufferable, and left England in 1796; he would make one last stay there in 1799. In
Hamburg he drew more advantage from his skill at billiards
than from his mastery of the violin. Yet his billiard playing did
not prevent him, in 1802 at the age of fifty-seven, from
astonishing his audiences in Berlin by the firmness of his bowing. In St. Petersburg he disappointed no one, even after Rode.
"The gaiety and elegance of his style even made it said that
with eyes closed one would have thought him the younger,"
writes Abbé Robineau, a violinist of great ability himself. It
was in St. Petersburg that Jarnovick ended a career which had
brought him there several times. He had been such a success in
1783 that Catherine the Great had ordered her director of
entertainments to offer him a contract. He was engaged with
an annual stipend of 3,000 rubles, while his wife, whose existence is thus revealed to us, received 2,000 rubles as an actress in
the French troupe at the court. He remained in St. Petersburg
until 1786, the period of his trip to Vienna and other places.
He was there again in 1789 (not for long, since he gave concerts in Basel the next year, and from 1791 to 1796 in the
British Isles, and in Germany at various times between 1786
and 1802). Three months after his last concert, death surprised
him there on November 23, 1804, while he was playing billiards.

He was given a beautiful funeral. Koslowsky composed

the music, which was performed in the Catholic church; Mme. Mara sang, surrounded by a picked chorus. Soon thereafter, in January 1805, Woldemar, Lolli's pupil, published a fine obituary article in the *Correspondance des professeurs et des musiciens*. Then oblivion advanced with measured step and carefully covered him with the veil it reserves for virtuosos.

However, Jarnovick was too good a musician to deserve such a prompt disaffection. Testimonials of admiration for him as a performer come from good judges.

La Borde saw in him "one of the most agreeable violinists that have ever existed . . . who astonishes more each time one hears him. No one has ever had more facility and technique than he, nor a more brilliant bow." Michael Kelly, the famous singer of Mozart's works, who knew all the virtuosos of his day, and Dittersdorf, one of the most celebrated violinists, praised not only his facility but the charm and grace of his playing. The contrabassist, Dragonetti, Viotti's friend and often his partner, declared one day that Jarnovick was the most elegant violinist to be heard before Paganini.

These qualities of elegance, charm, and delicacy also gave merit to his compositions. He had more instinct than knowledge. While he was in Vienna in 1786 he had Gyrowetz write his tuttis and the accompanying parts of his concertos. But his thematic invention was generous and ingenious, even though the development was weak and formalistic. The romances, which he was one of the first to substitute for the adagio movements, wonderfully reflect the sensibilities of his time— songs without words for drawing-room shepherds. In the *Encyclopédie Méthodique* published in 1791 during Jarnovick's life, a far-sighted critic, Ginguené, defined his concertos in this way:

"Jarnovick, whose witty, amiable, and graceful playing has been for several years the charm of our concerts, had for the same reason as Lolli [more imagination than profundity], the same indifference to the adagios, and since his independent spirit chafed under an uncomfortable yoke, he sometimes went so far as to omit them altogether. This was not the only novelty he introduced into the concerto. He made its style in general less noble and magnificent, but more flowing and graceful, more within reach of the audience; and always adroitly weaving into his most difficult passages a simple and popular melody, he created a genre which soon became the fashion. The composition of pieces in this style requiring less intelligence, less talent, and less knowledge, and their execution being also less demanding and easier, one heard nothing, one liked nothing but his concertos, or those of his imitators. Although he was not the first to use the rondo for the last movement, it is he who made a more frequent and more agreeable use of it, and it is to him especially that we owe this third change in the form of the concerto.

And Ginguené goes on to say that there was sometimes misuse of these rondos, "whose melody almost always has more of the character of a song than of instrumental music, as if we ended our grand operas with a drinking song, or heard an air of the streets at the end of *Dido* or *Iphigenia*."

On the whole, the concertos of Jarnovick, eclipsed overnight by those of Viotti, are not so clearly inferior as one might think. They have merit, or they approach it, in their technical maturity; and good masters, Baillot among others, recommended them. Their construction is rather simple; there again Viotti does not shine with too bright a light. The differ-

ence between them and the reason for their very dissimilar
fortunes is less in the artistic quality of the music than in the
sentiment it inspires, the one heroic and virile, animated by a
sort of revolutionary enthusiasm, in the style of the times that
were coming; the other, light, tender, superficial, in greater
and greater disharmony with the growing exaltation of the
public.

And here the romantic biographer would meet a rather
troubling enigma. There is a general tendency to establish an
analogy between the character of the composer and that of his
work, between the personality of a performer and his style of
playing.

Now Jarnovick, in his works and in his playing, so measured, so charming, so delicate, appears to us in life bizarre,
churlish, uncultivated. He passes his time in destroying the
friendships which come his way, dissipating the money his
talent earns for him. Conscious of his inability to avert the
blows of fortune, he provokes them, "carving his own misery,"
in the profound words applied to him by William Parke.

All is not tragic in the innumerable anecdotes related by his
contemporaries. He has on occasion a humorous insolence. One
day he announces a concert in Lyons at six francs a ticket. Few
music-lovers respond. Seeing this, he postpones the concert
until the next day, with seats at three francs each. This time
there is a crowd, but Jarnovick does not appear at the hour of
the concert; he has left town in revenge for the stinginess of
the people of Lyons. At the office of the publisher, Bailleux,
he breaks a pane of glass by mistake. "If you break windows
you pay for them," shouts Bailleux. "That's fair," replies
Jarnovick, "what do I owe you?" "Thirty sous." "Wait,

here's three livres." "But I haven't any change!" "Well, now
we're quits!" replies Jarnovick, breaking another pane. All is
well as long as his caprice spends itself against inanimate objects. This is not often the case, and Jarnovick's quarrelsome
disposition leads him to brawls, even to duels. "At the last
concert given by the Baron de Bagge," recounts Métra in his
Correspondance secrète of February 22, 1777, "the two famous
violinists Jarnovick and Pieltain quarrelled, accusing each other
of playing out of tune. Pieltain struck Jarnovick, who leapt
on the aggressor and scratched him with his fingernails; people
tried to separate them; the defender having only his teeth free,
used them to grab the end of Pieltain's nose. The Prince de
Guémenée, to whom both of the musicians belong, at first
enjoined them not to fight a duel, but as he was told that things
would come to that sooner or later, he consented with the
condition that he name the witnesses . . . Pieltain was
wounded rather painfully, but not dangerously. A reconcilia-
tion between the two musicians was solemnly made, to the
great satisfaction of all music-lovers; it seems sincere."

Through another escapade soon afterwards, Jarnovick in-
curred the disfavor of the Prince de Guémenée. Later he provoked Saint-Georges, the most accomplished fencer of his
time, going so far as to slap him. Saint-Georges turned toward
a witness and said simply: "I love his talent too much to fight
with him!"

In London, Shaw, the conductor of the Drury Lane orchestra, barely escaped the duel Jarnovick sought. Kelly tells the
story: "I used my influence to reconcile them. Jarnovick
knew not a word of English, Shaw not a word of French. Both
agreed on me as an arbitrator. I translated as faithfully as pos-

sible. Unhappily, Shaw, replying to one of Jarnovick's complaints, said 'Pooh Pooh.' 'Sacredieu!', exclaimed Jarnovick. 'What does this pooh! pooh! mean? Pooh! pooh! I won't listen to another word until you've translated pooh! pooh!' My desire to bring them together was frustrated for a time because I truly did not know how to put this 'pooh! pooh!' into French or Italian. In the end I succeeded in making them friends again."

Toward Cramer, on the other hand, Jarnovick was so in-insulting and refused him satisfaction so insolently, that he had to leave London in 1796 under a cloud of unanimous disapprobation. Mme. Bochsa, the niece of Mme. de Genlis, in her *Mémoires sur l'impératrice Joséphine*, tells us of another of his London exploits: "He was giving a concert; the hall was full; he begins his concerto, and seeing that the whispering continues, that the noise of cups and spoons does not cease, he turns toward the orchestra and says in a loud voice: 'Stop, my friends. These people don't understand anything about the arts. I am going to give them something suitable to their taste; it will always be good enough for people who drink hot water!' And he immediately played *J'ai du bon tabac*. What is amusing is that he was showered with applause, that the second piece was very well attended to, and that the tea-cups did not circulate until he had finished."

With Viotti, his arrogance almost capitulated. They had matched their talents the first time in Berlin, and Viotti had carried the day. When they found themselves both in London in 1792, Jarnovick brusquely accosted his rival and said, "I've had something against you for a long time; let's skip the quarrel, take up our violins, and we shall see who is Caesar and who is Pompey." Defeated again, he did not lose countenance but cried, "My word, my dear Viotti, it must be admitted that only the two of us know how to play the violin!"

It was again through hatred of a rival, Salomon, that he was guilty of gross impoliteness toward the Queen of England. She had manifested a wish to hear Jarnovick. He arrived for the concert, May 2, 1795, at York House; but seeing his enemy, he took to his heels, abandoning the audience, Queen, lords and all.

His learning was no better than his manners. The oboist, W. T. Parks, found himself in Jarnovick's company in Hampstead. Jarnovick could not pronounce the name of the street he lived on, in spite of the years he had lived in England, and tried in vain to make himself understood by his coachman. It was only when he was in complete despair that the idea came to him of singing the tune of *Malbrough*, so that his friends could direct the cab to Marlborough Street.

Illiterate in English, he was hardly less so in French. I possess one of his letters, addressed to his daughter, with such fantastic spelling that I have thought it best to accompany it with a translation.*

This sixth of March, 1791
My dear daughter,

I think you must be terribly occupied with your harpsichord because I have not had a letter from you in such a long time. That does not prevent me from writing to you to let you know what has happened to me. Do not expect good news because I have only bad news to send you. When I arrived in Dublin, Dr. Clarke came

---

* In the French version M. Pincherle prints in parallel columns Jarnovick's incredible original and a translation into decent French.—*Translator's note.*

to see me. I expected to see a man of a certain age. Not at all, I see a young man of around twenty-four years, who is a doctor of music without a doubt, under the protection of the viceroy, who doesn't know any better. A week before the first concert, I see in the papers that it is announced under the direction of Dr. Clarke and of Mr. Janiewicz. Being greatly surprised, I went to the Doctor and told him that my contract was under the direction of Dr. Clarke, and not Mr. Janiewicz. He replied that he had associated himself with Mr. Janiewicz to divide the risks of the enterprise. I replied that Mr. Janiewicz had neither the means to answer for my money nor the reputation to be my director, and that I would not play under his direction. You know my character: I lost my temper and wanted to go to law. But friends who read my contract have advised me to do nothing because the laws of this country permit any man who goes into an enterprise to associate himself with anyone he pleases, and that it was the fault of the person who made the contract not to have explained it. Seeing myself trapped like a mouse, and reflecting on my bad situation, I said to myself, "If I take off, I shall be like a man who steals his subscribers' money," and reflecting on my honor and that of my poor family, I submitted to my fate. Some time later I found myself with the Doctor and Mr. Janiewicz. I told them that they were scoundrels to have taken advantage of my good faith, and if it weren't for the law I should take them by the nose and give them a good thrashing. They received my compliment like the scoundrels that they are, and have made many cabals against me. I have kept to myself; I played at the four concerts, which were filled as never before; they gained an immense sum of money, and I had the pain of seeing them divide the spoils.

The day of my benefit arrived, it having been put off three times; there was a sort of rebellion against Parliament, and no one dared go out in the streets, so that they took in only forty-seven guineas at my concert. In my unhappiness, I had the pleasure of seeing that they will be obliged to disburse two hundred guineas! You see from all that, dear Mimi, that your father is not happy, and having only 150 guineas in all, it is impossible for me to do honor to my affairs in London. That is why I shall take the course of not returning there until I can settle my affairs honorably. I shall tell you of my plans, and when you can rejoin me with little Sophie. In the meantime, tomorrow I shall send you some money which I advise you to spend very carefully. Goodbye, my dear Mimi. I embrace you tenderly, and little Sophie as well, and give you both my blessing.

Your father,
GIORNOVICHI.

Give me news of my affairs and do not speak to anyone about my intentions, for I am afraid of being arrested here; that is why I do not count on staying much longer. Try to give me some news of Mérote, for I am fearful that if she returns to London, coming from Paris, they will make her leave England, as people tell me. That would be paying very dear for the foolish thing she did, after having been in prison for six months. The very idea desolates me; that is why, in spite of all the pleasure I should take in seeing her again, I should prefer for the moment that she stay with her mother until my affairs improve; I would have sent her what money I could for her living expenses, being persuaded that she will conduct herself like an honest woman. Goodbye, my dear child.

My dear Mimi, I have just received your letter at the moment I was going to send this one off, and I have hurried to find a little more money to add to what I was going to send you, so that you could send some to poor Mérote. But I am afraid that the money will arrive too late, or that it will be lost on the way. Poor woman! I fear for her situation, for I am afraid that when she arrives at Dover they will not let her pass, or that they will put her in prison. That is why this idea came to me: if you went to Mme. the Duchess of Devonshire and told her my worries on the subject of Mérote so that she might have the kindness to give her a passport to the Duke of Portland, to whom she is related, I think that she would do it because she has a kind heart. However, if you find another way, use it. Look, go to see Austin and ask him also to write to Pleyel to send her the ten louis. Then she can leave with these ten louis from Paris to Calais, and in Calais she should find the fifteen guineas that I am sending you for her. Look, my dear Mimi, do the best you can. I am sending you now twenty-seven guineas, and with the two that you should have received from Mme. Mara, that makes twenty-nine in all. You send fifteen to Mérote, and fourteen remain for you. Pay Sophie's wetnurse, and use the rest for yourself and your lodging with great care, for God knows how affairs will turn out in such critical times as we are in. The money that I am sending you is not payable for some time, but you can have it discounted for a few shillings. Austin will tell you that. Go to the aid of Mérote as soon as you can, for we are honor bound to get her out of trouble. Goodbye, my dear child, I embrace you and Sophie and give you both my blessing— and am your affectionate father

GIORNOVICHI.

Reply as soon as you receive my letter, so that I shall know if you have received the money.

I had promised a mystery to the biographer who took Jarno-vick as a subject. This letter is full of it. We know Clarke, the conductor; Janiewicz, a violinist of great talent, in spite of what our hero says, who had a great success at the Concert Spirituel (December 25, 1787); Mme. Mara, the singer; and Ignace Pleyel, the composer. But who suspected the existence of Mimi, of Sophie, of Mérote? So the unhappy wanderer had a family in tow! Hemmed in by creditors, ruined by bad luck, he also had to provide for a woman just out of prison and who ran the risk of being thrown in again, and for two girls, one of whom was very young. Underneath Jarnovick's successes, his fame, his boasting, a foundation of misery and anguish, a losing struggle against himself, against this unfortunate character that he recognized and could not subdue.

The comedy of his jargon fades before the sadness it expresses, and one is full of pity for the poor devil trapped in his unhappy fate, "carving his own misery. . . ."

ALEXANDER BOUCHER

"An artist unique in his field, original even in his imitations, the inimitable chief of the romantic school in musical art, Alexander Boucher was beyond a doubt the first violinist of our century, not only in France but also in Europe."

This declaration closes the 245th and last page of a volume on Alexander Boucher published in 1890 by Gustave Vallat. It contains some surprising statements: "chief of the romantic school, beyond a doubt the first violinist in Europe"? If that were so, it would be known, as the saying goes. But more than one cultivated reader is ignorant even of the name of the hero cited above, for which he cannot be blamed.

Thus two extremes oppose each other: the official biographer, completely absorbed in his subject; and the musical public, equally mistaken—and totally uninterested. However reluctant one may be to fish for the truth between two waters, at an equal distance from contrasting errors, it must be said that that is where the truth lies, and not elsewhere, and for all that he was not Paganini, Schumann, Berlioz or Liszt, Boucher remains nevertheless a person of marked interest.

Our intention is not to recount the adventurous life of our violinist, thereby repeating the book which has been devoted to him. We shall make a very brief summary of the incontrovertible facts it presents. Our interest lies in verifying certain points on which we have information coming from sources other than Boucher's personal notes or his widow's recollections, on which Gustave Vallat founded his panegyric; and in seeing what can be deduced of the true personality of Alexander Boucher.

He was born in Paris on April 11, 1778, on the Rue St.-Maur, the son of an ex-musician of the Grey Musketeers of Louis XV, who had been noticed by the Marquis de Jumilhac and taken on as his secretary-steward. From his earliest years the little Alexander showed himself to be prodigiously gifted in music. He was six years old when Marie Antoinette asked to hear him play. He was brought to Versailles. He passed proudly through the ranks of servants "who in spite of their arrogant mien did not overawe him." (So said Boucher, according to Vallat.) The queen was captivated. "Ah!" she exclaimed, "what a lovely child! What an alert expression! What an open face! How happy his mother must be to have such a beautiful little boy, so healthy and so intelligent!"

This little boy fell in love there with a little girl, Céleste Gallyot (one of the companions of the princess, Madame Royale), whom he asked in marriage in all seriousness, and whom, much later, he was to marry.

Separated from her one fine day, in the course of their youthful engagement, he threw himself into looking for her, weeping and calling her name as he ran all over the park of Versailles and the forest of Satory, where he fell into exhausted sleep. He was found at dawn the next day. "Thus at the age of six years, Alexander Boucher loved to the point of folly and revealed in his passion all the transports of an ardent and unconquerable nature . . ."

Meanwhile he pursued his violin studies, under various masters, Subrin de Sainte-Marie, then Gaviniès, who, again in the words of Gustave Vallat, acclaimed him in these ringing terms: "This child, a veritable little prodigy, is destined to become one of the first artists of the century. Bring him to me: I want to direct his studies, to aid him to develop his precocious genius, and my task will be all the easier because he truly has the sacred fire."

He worked with Guillaume Navoigille, who entered him in the Lycée des Arts, founded by Madame de Mortaigne, and soon took him on tour to Orléans, then to Bourges, where the archbishop insisted on taking him into his care. On his mother's insistence, the little Alexander returned to Paris as the Revolution approached.

To believe his story, he played a role of the first importance in the events that overturned Europe. Gustave Vallat shows him assiduously following the discussions that took place in his home on the burning question of the new doctrines, "avid to enrich his spirit with the truths which they [his father and his friends] proclaimed and to fill his soul with the generous sentiments that the love of the public good inspired in him. . . . In the moral sphere, Alexander was no longer a child; he felt growing in him [at the age of eleven!] those strong passions that alone propel men to great ends. But in the physical sense he was still weak."

Six months of training in a nearby barracks, and a metamorphosis took place: "Alexander developed under their very eyes at a prodigious rate; he grew tall, his chest became larger, his limbs became stronger every day; his muscles already had almost the strength of steel . . ." Thus he put himself at the head of his comrades from the Lycée des Arts, teaching them the hard trade of bearing arms, and we see him "embracing the cause of the Revolution with all the ardor of his nature." He takes part in the storming of the Bastille, "always in the forefront, happy to be among the first to brave the peril," and it is he, who, astride the back of a sergeant, seizes the text of the capitulation as it is handed out through a loophole. All of which does not prevent him from seeing with enviable precision a mass of things of which the historians of the Revolution say not a word.

There appears here a characteristic trait of the psychology of Alexander Boucher that Vallat does not comment on, but which we shall encounter many times: it is the facility, one might almost say the spontaneity, with which he arranges, modifies, and interprets events to appear to his advantage. For here is the supplication he addresses twenty-six years later to the Duke of Orléans. (It is a large folded sheet, dictated by Boucher, corrected and signed by him, and it carries in the margin a very favorable recommendation from the Mayor of Fontainebleau, Du Bois d'Arnouville):

To His Royal Highness the Duke of Orléans.

Alexander-Jean de Boucher (born in Paris in 1778), former director of music and first violinist at the former Court of Spain, honorary member of the Swiss Confederation of Music, of several academies and learned societies, etc., has the honor to inform Your Highness that he ardently desires to gratify his love for the august family of the Bourbons. Fleeing the Revolution at the age of sixteen, he took refuge in Spain where His Christian Majesty King Charles IV received him with a special welcome and at-

tached him to his suite; this generous monarch judging that he was
destined to add to the glory of his state, deigned further to consider him under other aspects and even to honor him with his intimate friendship!

Having since returned to his native land for reasons of health
which prevented him from going back to Spain, and although no
longer belonging to This Good King, at the time of his troubles
he thought only of his attachment to the family of august Bourbons! in the impossibility of giving useful proofs to our legitimate
princes of France he devoted himself anew to his feeling for the
Unfortunate Charles IV and returned to France expressly on the
arrival of this prince at Fontainebleau to offer him his life, conse-
crating his whole existence and that of his numerous family (he
did not even want to accept any compensation or payment which
the generous Charles IV insisted that he accept). Thus it was that
he had the courage to be the only Frenchman who dared to bring
him consolation when everyone abandoned him, not fearing to
speak to him (in the presence of the Napoleonic Court which was
there by order) and to sleep not far from Charles IV the better
to watch over his precious days! This action was very dangerous
at a time when one dared not even pronounce the name of a
Bourbon. It was noted and as a reward for this exemplary devotion, the worthy Bourbon, moved to tears by this evidence of
courage and fidelity which later cost me years of proscription,
publicly told me then, before the authorities, pressing me to his
heart: "Come to my arms, I know your sentiments, never leave
me," etc., etc. . . . These august words have been recorded, even
in the newspapers of the time to the extent that circumstances permitted. They are exact and in the knowledge of all those who
heard them pronounced by Charles IV at Fontainebleau (and
attested by the aforesaid Mayor of the city). From that moment
Charles IV desired the said Boucher to take up service again near
his sacred person. And no one dared separate them until that
monarch left for Rome. The suppliant was then designed as prin-

cipal victim, as well as his numerous family whose devotion was the cause of their ruin. He had the painful glory of being the first on the list which proscribed by name each of the old and faithful servants to whom the King was attached and without any regard for this venerable monarch, the model of so many assembled virtues!!! The undersigned had the further distinction of being one of that small number of Frenchmen who have never petitioned any but the son of Saint-Louis, nor wished to serve any but this august family. For which conduct the suppliant hopes that your Royal Highness will deign to distinguish him by admitting him to his service either as first musician or in any other post, according to his capacity be it also as secretary. He has for a wife one of the greatest talents recognized in Europe, of a deportment and education so distinguished that she was chosen to teach the Infantas of Spain. She was also in France as Lady-in-Waiting to the Queen, and was first harpist and pianist in the orchestra of Good King Charles.

It is for these reasons that the suppliant dares appeal to the protector of the Arts in France, and especially because of the invariable character of his acts of courageous devotion and the fidelity that he showed in perilous times from pure devotion to the august Bourbons whom he loved and cherished.

While awaiting this special grace, Monseigneur, he has the honor of being your Royal Highness's most respectful and faithful servant.

Alexander Boucher

Rue Duphot n.6, near the Assumption Saint-Honoré. Paris, the 19th October, 1814

This petition is rather hard to reconcile with Boucher's precocious revolutionary zeal: one might let it pass, and attribute to the impetuosity of youth a short-lived predilection for the ideas of 1789, if at a very advanced age our musician

had not called on it again. In April 1848 there took place in
Paris a general assembly of artists and musicians, called to
elect one of its members as a delegate to the government. The
Gazette musicale of April 23, 1848, gives this account: "M.
Alexander Boucher appeared first in the speaker's stand: fate
had decided it thus. The veteran of the violin said but few
words to witness his devotion to the cause of artists and to
pledge himself to defend it if it were entrusted to him. His
speech established clearly, as he himself said, that he handled
words less skillfully than the bow. He gave a proof of candor
which amused the assembly, in saying that he had always been
a republican since the fall of the Bastille, but that he had been
careful not to flaunt it under the preceding regimes!" And the
assembly elected Halévy.

Let us return to the story of Alexander at the dawn of the
Revolution: it is the period of his service in the National
Guard, where he receives, at the age of twelve, on September
7, 1790, a commission as a volunteer signed by Lafayette (the
same Lafayette would later give him an honorable discharge).
Adventures shower on him: the boy with muscles of steel
measures himself in a duel with an opponent thirty years old, a
professional fencer, whom he disarms; he marches in 1792 with
the columns which leave for Champagne; he fights "like a
lion" at Ste. Menehould; he falls ill. "Broken-hearted at not
being able to participate in the victory of Valmy, and nursing
the hope of taking his revenge in battle as soon as he regains
his strength," he tries to hide his illness from his parents. In
vain: he is brought back to Paris, where he seeks his fortune.
Passing in front of Viotti's house, he tries to get some lessons
from him. But he has the unhappy idea of playing for him a

piece by Mestrino, Viotti's most formidable rival. A dialogue ensues:

"Miserable child, braggart, scoundrel, you come here to mock me; you are sent by my rival to ask for lessons. You must be his favorite pupil, how else could you execute so well these pieces that bristle with difficulties? I am not your dupe, get out of here, and never come back, or I'll have you thrown out."

"But, Monsieur, you are mistaken, I swear that I do not know Mestrino; I have never seen him, never heard him."

"That is impossible."

Boucher persists and presents himself again, this time having studied the trios of Viotti, who marvels at his playing but does not give him the lessons he wants so much. Using a stratagem (poor Alexander in the course of his long career had to use and abuse many stratagems and devices) he introduces himself, as he is passing by his office, to the Viscount de Marin, a harpist and violinist of renown, and M. de Marin keeps him in work until the day comes when the Viscount must emigrate.

Life becomes difficult: Alexander enters the orchestra of the Théâtre du Palais on April 1, 1793 (the engagement is signed on March 21st). In his spare time he earns some money to help his family by playing patriotic airs in the taverns or for the dances at the customs barriers, wearing the red bonnet of the Revolution and dressed as a sans-culotte. Incidentally he saves the life of his benefactress, Madame de Mortaigne, when she appears before the Committee of Public Safety. "Citizens," he exclaims, "I come in the name of all my comrades, in the name of the entire Section of the Bonnet-Rouge, to which I have the honor to belong, I come to ask you to requisition, as useful to the arts and to our country, the life of the citizeness Mortaigne. She was formerly an aristocrat, I admit: The execution of the law against suspects has deprived her of her liberty, nothing could be more just. War to the death on conspirators! Let them be pursued unrelentingly, that is the cry of republicans; let these former nobles and suspects be taken off to prison, the safety of France requires it, etc., etc. . . ." There follows an exalted account of the services rendered by the citizeness Mortaigne to the education of youth, a eulogy of her civic spirit and her zeal. As a consequence, the Committee of Public Safety requisitions the citizeness Mortaigne and sets her free. Later Boucher also procures the freedom of the Marquise of Montgeroult, a celebrated pianist, and of Mlle. de Walbonne. For in the words of Gustave Vallat, this "new Amphion, thanks to the magic of his bow, had the gift of moving hearts of stone: by the variations that he improvised on the *Marseillaise* and on *Ça ira*, he charmed the obdurate Robespierre, tempered somewhat Couthon's savage disposition, softened for a moment the inexorable soul of Saint-Just."

On January 29, 1795, thanks to Carnot, he enters the Ministry of Finances, where Baillot is already employed. As a member of the orchestra at the Théâtre Feydeau, where he is also employed, he rubs shoulders with Rode and Kreutzer. He takes part, on the 13th Vendémiaire in the year IV, in an uprising by some sections of Paris against the Convention. Taken prisoner, he escapes and finds refuge in Madrid. His existence there is at first precarious; robbed by the blind beggars among whom he lives, he decides to end his life. "Loading a pistol which he had bought for this purpose, he presses it to his temple and pulls the trigger; the shot goes off . . ." and this young man so valiant in arms escapes, for he misses. But he has attracted attention and pity, and the judge charged with punishing him for his attempt at suicide shows him a way to approach the king, Charles IV, who is a violinist and mad about music. The account of the stratagem (again) to which he resorts to bring himself to the attention of the king, of his success, of his engagement as first violinist to the king and second violinist in the Royal Chapel orchestra is told at length by Gustave Vallat, evidently just as he found it in Alexander's notes. We are told that "Boucher's influence at Court was considerable. He could have been a minister, if he wished, such was the king's affection for him; but he was too wise to renounce his supremacy in the art where no one could dispute him." He left Spain when it became apparent that he had a chest disease, caused by overwork.

Another version of his departure is more widespread, that given for example by one of Boucher's contemporaries, the Baron de Trémont: "After having been for a long time first violinist to the king of Spain, Charles IV, he was dismissed by this prince who played the violin like a king, that is to say, very badly, and who thought he played well. In one of his concerts he played with Boucher, before his assembled court, a *symphonie concertante* in which he made a terrible racket, being twenty measures behind. At the end of the piece he loudly reproached Boucher for having missed his part. The poor Alexander had not the wit to submit to this reproach, just as he had not been enough of a courtier to follow the prince in his wanderings. He maintained that the fault was not his. His Majesty's musical *amour-propre*, always very strong, sent him into a truly royal fit of anger, and Boucher committed the blunder of leaving the hall. The furious Charles cried out 'Stop the rascal, the scoundrel . .' The violinist, after traversing several rooms, found his way barred in the last one by a row of halberdiers with pikes lowered. He was taken back to the prince who had regained his good humor and said to him: 'Ah, there you are, you rascal, another time pay more attention to your part.' "

What we know of Boucher's boasting inclines us to accept Trémont's version in preference to his own.

We find Boucher in Paris again, where a marriage falls through because he shuts himself up in his room for fifteen days hypnotized by the composition of "a *symphonie concertante* for two violins which he intended to perform on the eve of his wedding" and in which he pays homage to his fiancée. Thinking herself abandoned, the poor girl falls ill of chagrin and her parents brusquely dismiss the fiancé. All turns out for the best: at this crucial moment he meets once again his first love, Céleste Gallyot, of the Court of Versailles, whom he had last seen as a harpist at the Théâtre Feydeau and lost sight of during the events of Vendémiaire. Despair! She has been married in the meantime and is now Mme. Fages. Delirious joy! She is a widow! He marries her and together they begin a series of concert tours.

On May 4, 1806, he performs at the Opéra in Paris, during Catalani's first concert. It is a success, but the eccentricity of his playing calls forth the reproach of "juggling, buffoonery." He dreams of making a name beyond the Rhine. He arrives at Mainz on October 6, 1806. The next day the *Mainz Journal* publishes an announcement manifestly inspired, if not composed, by him: "We learn of the recent arrival in this city of the virtuoso, M. Alexander Boucher, a celebrated violinist, first soloist at the Court of Spain. It is not known how long he will stay here, but after the enthusiasm that this great musician has inspired everywhere he has made himself known (notably on his last trip to Holland), all connoisseurs of real talent in music will want to hear this rare player, who has not appeared before in our country, where he will be appreciated and enjoyed according to his merit."

I am inclined to attribute the writing of this announcement to Boucher, partly because of its style, and also because of his inveterate habit of sending letters, advice, and communications of all kinds to the newspapers. Gustave Vallat reproduces numerous examples, the newspapers of the period are full of them, and several original letters now in my possession bear witness to a letter-writing mania which became more and more extreme and unhealthy. I shall quote only one note, addressed May 7, 1840, to:

M. Virmaitre, lawyer, Rue de Bondy, n.7.

Sir and honored friend, several days ago the management of the newspaper *Le Corsaire* cut me off from my favorite reading, that great paper. Do me the kindness to tell me to what I should attribute this undeserved severity. If you do not know by what right I received the favor of a proof-sheet of this interesting journal I shall tell you and perhaps you will also think that the cashier of the *Corsaire* treats me like a pirate, and that in hitting this way at an old friend, in showing force rather than justice toward a poor musician, it is no longer musical. In a time of crisis I opened my purse like a friend to stand security for this paper and put forth my best efforts for it; I can, if necessary, furnish proofs, and documents, one of them signed by the estimable M. Viennot, your

worthy and respected father-in-law; there is my principal claim
to this goodwill: has it lapsed? Oblige me by telling me.

I do not think I should be mistakenly lumped together with
those who were indifferent or with the general public by the successors of the founders whom I also esteem having continued the
same kindness for a year (am still happy to procure subscribers
for our dear *Corsaire*).

I have the honor of being devotedly yours (and whatever the
outcome); greetings and brotherhood from the French artist, the
only one among the famous to be without the cross of honor, or
other distinctions than his own actions and the former friendship
of the good *Corsaire* on which he will always pride himself.

And this is signed, with a strange flourish full of sharps and
flats:

> Alexander Boucher
> Cosmopolitan artist.

and followed by a postscript:

If I am so attached to this brilliant *Corsaire*, it is because I draw
my inspiration from it, I renew there my artistic verve, my feeble
talents are perfected in adapting to my violin bits of its satires and
its clever sallies! (Happy products of its candid loyalty! So rare
elsewhere nowadays! . . .)

At other times Boucher would sign, enlarging his flourish
with three exclamation points:

> Your very honored Dean of the renowned musicians
> of Europe,
> Alexander Boucher,
last of the violinists formerly celebrated and first of the innovators

of today, ex-director of music at foreign courts, honored member of academies, etc., medalist of Sainte-Hélène, etc. . . .

Or more simply:

Nestor of famous musicians.

We have now shifted little by little from the domain of history to that of psychology: perhaps it will be more interesting to penetrate there, sending the reader seeking a chronological account to the biographical dictionaries or to the book by Gustave Vallat.

Parallel to Alexander's letter-writing mania goes his love of making speeches, although as can be seen from the excerpt cited above from the *Gazette musicale*, he was qualified neither by his education nor by any marked gift for oratory. We have seen him addressing the Committee of Public Safety. In Madrid he addresses a discourse to Charles IV to explain to him that he played the violin badly: "Sire, I do not ask to be released from my post, I resign. It grieves me to come to this cruel extremity, but it is absolutely essential that I cease to remain in Your Majesty's service. I am French, here is my national cockade that I wear on my heart, I show it to your eyes, it is my shield. The French are the masters of the world, they triumph in Africa as they have triumphed in Europe, and one does not level against them the weapon which serves to whip dogs. Up till now I have kept the most respectful silence, I was not at fault and did not wish to justify myself. I hoped that Your Majesty would deign to understand my language of silence. Now I have broken my chains, I am free and I am going to tell the King of Spain the truth which one always hides from sovereigns: a man can make peace and make war, wisely govern an empire, in a word, have all the virtues of a great ruler, and, like other men, be subject to certain distractions, light enough without doubt, but which suffice to make trouble in his playing of a musical passage." Upon which the King of all the realms of Spain embraces him effusively—according to the account which Boucher himself recorded for future historians.

He harangues the passers-by on the boulevards during the Hundred Days; he averts a riot by delivering a stirring eulogy at the funeral of General Foy; in May 1848 he presents himself at the Hôtel de Ville and reads to the members of the Provisional Government, in the name of "the veterans of the storming of the Bastille," a speech of felicitation for having "restored the honor of our France, so degraded by the regime just overturned."

At concerts he apostrophises the artists whose playing pleases him. At the second concert given by Ernst, in Marseilles, in 1836, he rises from the first row of the amphitheater where he had been sitting. "Young man," he cries in a ringing voice, "you play like Paganini!" The anonymous writer who reports this in the review *Provence* in 1883 also tells us how, in the course of a comedy which was given before the concert, Boucher had provided the public with some unexpected amusement: the spectators were disrupting an unsuccessful scene with their jibes, the hall was becoming riotous, "but soon all eyes are directed toward a graying head which wagged feverishly to the accompaniment of two long arms waving like semaphores. Alexander Boucher is recognized and on every side he is urged to speak. This promises to be more amusing than the interrupted play. Boucher rises, composes himself, and assumes a Napoleonic pose: "Ladies and gentlemen, all artists are honorable . . . why should we not listen to the gentlemen of the comedy? Literature and music walk hand in hand . . . Certainly, like you, I want to hear the concert, but I think that literature also has its charm. So let us quiet ourselves and allow the play to proceed."

The audience had laughed so hard during this solemnly delivered speech that it was disarmed against the poor vaudeville and let it finish in peace.

At a concert in 1846 at which Alard played, "a rather strange incident occurred which touched, or at least amused, the audience: a violinist formerly celebrated, Alexander Boucher, called Alexander of the Violinists, flung himself on Alard's neck and embraced him with tender emotion; I think that he even shed some tears. The next day someone asked Boucher if he thought he had pleased Alard: 'My friend,' he replied in a grave voice, 'he played admirably, he deserved it!' " At the age of eighty he still climbed over the seats at the concert hall of the Conservatory to give the accolade to the players.

These anecdotes reflect an assurance, a naive self-contentment which the vicissitudes of his career never altered, as the letters he wrote his wife after his concerts abroad testify, even more clearly than the speeches Vallat reproduced:

"My concert succeeded beyond all my hopes. You can have no idea. Enthusiasm is general. I am harassed on all sides. The difficulties of organization are immense, because I have enemies at Court. But I have confounded them, for I distinguished myself as never before in my life." (Mainz, November 1806.)

". . . But in the adagio of my quartet in C, that adagio which I play, as you know, almost all on the E string, the string breaks . . . I quickly catch what remains of it with my mouth, as it would have bothered me by lying on the other strings, and I keep on as if none were missing, just as I did in Rotterdam and so many other times in my life. You should have seen the musicians, their mouths open in admiration, and all the audience coming closer to hear better, and even more to see if I would make mistakes. You know that I do not lose my head in a crisis. I redouble my attention and care, I reassure everyone modestly, and in this way I obtain the approbation of all. Prudence and moderation assure the success of all great talents. This incident served me well; for I came out of it appearing simpler and better, and especially more within the reach of those ears which are not used to hearing me." (Frankfurt, December 1, 1806.) In August 1813 Rode arrived in Bern just as Boucher was going to give a concert. Boucher, on Rode's refusal, played alone. "I do not think," writes Boucher, "that you have ever seen me so calm, so equal to my best, in a word, so perfect; Rode [who was there simply as a member of the audience] grew paler each instant . . ." In June 1814, after having played in London: "They say . . . that if I come back next winter I will cause a musical revolution. They do not hesitate to say (here they are without affectation and one can speak out on any subject in this country of the true, frank, and good liberty in the best sense) that Viotti has never been my equal."

Spohr recounts in his memoirs that Boucher gave him a letter of introduction to the Baron d'Assignies, at Lille, and that the Baron later showed it to him as a curiosity. It included this pronouncement: "If I am, as they say, the Napoleon of violinists, Spohr is the Moreau."

If the title "Napoleon of violinists" seems a little out of line, Boucher had rather good reason to use it; he resembled the Emperor physically, as one of his contemporaries, the violinist Blondeau, tells us, "to the point where more than once he troubled the quiet security of the Restoration," and a German historian, Friedrich Rassmann, calls him Boucher-Bonaparte (Alexander) and adds in a note: "So called because of his extraordinary resemblance to Napoleon."

Our man had made a considerable element of publicity out of wearing from time to time a little hat and a gray field coat copied after those of his illustrious model. Thus disguised, he inspired a crowd of loiterers to work on the fortifications during the Hundred Days. He even proposed to the Emperor that he put him at the head of an army corps where he would impersonate him, being directed from behind the scenes by a military man. "The false Napoleon appearing at positions far removed from those where the real one showed himself, could, in case of defeat, revive the courage of the soldiers, and might, by his very presence, put the enemy to flight." The proposition was not taken up. For the rest, Napoleon had for a long time been irritated by this resemblance: the memoirs of the Duchess d'Abrantès tell how he became angry in the presence of the musician for this very reason.

Twice after 1820 Boucher had occasion to impersonate the Emperor. The Grand Duke Nicholas had invited him to lunch, and to entertain the company he had some marches composed by Boucher played out of doors. There was a frost hard enough to crack stones, and Boucher suffered at the thought of what the musicians were enduring. The Grand Duke at first refused his request to have them come indoors.

"Then Boucher rises, and pointing to his protégés while he fixes the Prince with a strange look, he says in a strong, deep voice: 'Grant me this favor, I beg you.' It was the gesture, the look, the tone, of Napoleon. There was something haughty and imperious in that request. The Grand Duke was as if hypnotized: he thought he saw and heard again the man who had made all the sovereigns of the world tremble, and he yielded, in spite of his obstinate pride: he submitted to a force greater than himself."

Soon afterward, the Empress of Russia asked him to "be Napoleon." According to the diarists of the day, he accepted without hesitation. According to Boucher, in Vallat's account, the affair took another turn. He began by protesting: "I am an artist and nothing else. To imitate Napoleon, to expose him to indiscreet public curiosity, what can I say? Only a mountebank would make him a laughing-stock for your subjects. Reflect also, Madame, that it concerns an unfortunate hero, a dead man."

"I want my Napoleon, I must have him, and to get him, I can think of a way which will prevail over your reluctance. I shall conduct you . . ."

"To Siberia?"

"No, into my study; choose those persons who can be admitted to this private sitting, and let us begin."

"The Empress took the violinist by the arm, he chose the Grand Dukes and the Prince of Modena. The door of the private room was hardly shut before the princes wanted to divest Boucher of his clothes so that he could put on the costume required by the occasion. But Boucher stopped them with a gesture and said firmly: 'No masquerade. You wanted to see Napoleon? Here he is!'

"He then directed toward the Empress and her sons a look of hurt pride which made them withdraw into themselves, and toward the Prince of Modena a look of profound scorn, disconcerting to this Frenchman who had gone over to the Russian army. Such is the lesson Boucher knew how to give to people in high places who were forgetful of propriety, and to this nobleman who had forgotten his honor."

Spohr also tells in his memoirs that "Boucher had studiously copied the bearing of the exiled Emperor, wearing his hat in the same way, and he even had the same manner of taking a pinch of snuff with the utmost precision. While on tour, when he arrived in a city where he was not yet known, he immediately presented himself with his acquired mannerisms on the public promenade or at the theater to attract the attention of the public and get himself talked about; he even tried to spread the story that he was persecuted by the present king of France and banished because of this resemblance to Napoleon, since it brought back the memory of the adored exile in the hearts of the people. At Lille, at any rate, where I later learned this," continues Spohr, "he announced his concert in this fashion: 'An unhappy resemblance forces me to live as an expatriate; before leaving my beloved country I shall give one last farewell concert, etc.' "

Boucher's version is not entirely unbelievable: one can very well imagine this whimsical artist indulging spontaneously in an imitation which aggrandized him in his own eyes, but balking at the obligation to travesty himself at a command. There

is in him a quasi-permanent mixture of braggadocio and true
dignity. He took part, with his wife, in a royal concert given
in 1817. Almost a year later, he was invited to present himself
to the Secretariat of Light Entertainment to collect . . . 75
francs. He protests, judging with good reason that the sum was
not worthy of his talents, nor his wife's. But he ends his letter
of refusal to the Duke d'Aumont, Gentleman of the King's
Bedchamber, in these words:

"To refuse is to impose on myself a triple privation, since
in spite of the meagerness of my fortune and the expenses of
supporting a family, I had earmarked the best part of what is
due me for the relief of the unfortunates shipwrecked on the
Medusa, to the erection of a statue to good King Henry, and
to the proposed monument to the immortal author of *Tartuffe*
and *The Miser* . . ."

In June 1823 Prince Galitzin of Russia, shocked that
Boucher had refused an invitation, wrote him the following
letter:

"Prince V. Galitzin asks M. Boucher to send the book of
quartets which he needs today: and since for some time in the
future he will not be making any music and until the departure
of M. Bouché [*sic*] he will probably not have the pleasure of
hearing him again, he sends him herewith 150 rubles for the
evening he spent with him on June 21st last. He begs him to
accept the expression of his regards." Boucher wrote a note
justifying himself, and added in a postscript: "It is purely out
of a sense of delicacy that I do not return the 150 rubles; I beg
Your Excellency to be persuaded that no motive of self-in-
terest brought me to your presence, I am generous in actions
as in sentiments."

This generosity was not a myth. Although it was often sullied by a touch of the theatrical, it was none the less effective. One cannot count the number of violinists begging on street corners for whom Boucher, by borrowing their violin and passing the hat (with great eloquence), assured copious takings.

Boucher was capable of interrupting a concert tour to organize a series of benefits for the reconstruction of a city razed by fire, of lending in any circumstances his gracious help to whoever asked for it. We have seen him intervene with the Grand Duke Nicholas whose caprice made musicians play outdoors in zero weather. Spohr found in him, when he met him in Brussels in 1820, not a jealous rival but a friend, eager to help in the organization of his concert.

These various traits of character will perhaps help us to understand a very real talent, at the start of his career full of magnificent promise, but which nevertheless fell into the shadow of oblivion even during Boucher's lifetime. The critic Scudo could write sadly in 1860: "The series of public concerts ended with that given by M. Alexander Boucher, veteran violinist and conjurer."

There is no doubt that Boucher achieved while very young a transcendent virtuosity: the impression produced on Charles IV, articles in journals before our musician undertook the systematic conquest of men of letters, all that we know of his youth confirms the judgment of the *Correspondance des professeurs et des amateurs de musique* in 1804: "An irreproachable correctness of intonation, even in double stopping, from the end of the fingerboard to the bridge, whether ascending or descending, the dynamic gradations, the drawing out and

connecting of tones by turns brilliant or soft and moving, infinite variety in bowing, a profound mastery of the fingerboard
of the instrument, double cadence [double trill], aplomb, wisdom—in a word, M. Boucher has had time to show he possesses
all the qualities that are the mark of a good school." In 1805,
the young Camille Pleyel, an excellent judge in the matter,
writing to his mother from Vienna, set down these impressions
(which are preserved in the archives of the Société Pleyel):
". . . We went the day before yesterday to Ellmenreich's,
where we played some of papa's quartets, which were never
played better . . . ; the first violinist has great fire and plays
in the genre of Boucher, but has nowhere near his technique."

We know that many years later Boucher had the honor of
being cordially received by Beethoven, who gave him as a
souvenir (now in the Library of the Paris Conservatory) a
musical autograph, two staves of music, with this dedication:
"Written on the 29th of April, 1822, as M. Boucher, the great
violinist, has done me the honor of paying me a visit. Ludwig
van Beethoven." Acknowledged masters such as Mendelssohn,
Liszt, Weber, Lesueur, Berlioz, Rossini, treated him, if not as
an equal, at least as an artist worthy of consideration. In April
1828 his situation being rather strained by a series of con-
tretemps brought on by the ill will of the administration of the
Beaux-Arts, a subscription for his benefit was opened by the
Figaro. Among the subscribers were Lesueur, Boieldieu, Ca-
rafa, Plantade, Tulou, de Bériot, Mlle. Mars, and the élite of
the artistic world.

Master of his instrument as he was, with a certain gift of
communicating emotion, an appearance which ingratiated him
with the public in advance, and influential friends who were

ready to make everything easy for him, how can we explain the series of mortifications that overtook his career in his mature years?

By the too exact conformity of his private personality, if one can call it that, and his musical personality. In both there is the same lack of restraint, the same intrusion of fantasy which does not know how to limit itself and overshoots its goal. Charlatanism in the production of his concerts. Spohr, who had nothing against him and recognized his great qualities, shows him pompous and being waited on by his wife: "When he had seated himself for the quartet, she asked him for the key to his violin case, opened the case, brought him the violin, then the bow which she had already rubbed with rosin; finally she placed the music in front of him and sat down to turn the pages." He would change violins according to whether he was playing an adagio or a fast movement, taking a bow with black hairs for the strong passages. Eccentricity penetrated even his playing. In Vienna, where he gave a series of concerts, the *Wiener Musikzeitung* called his virtuosity "so break-neck that it takes on a half-comic character. It pleases him to play with the bow held the wrong way around, under the bridge, or with the violin behind his back," like Franz Clement. He caused his wife, whose musical taste was purer than his, to play a duet for piano and harp, the piano played with the left hand and the harp with the right.

The reactions of the public ran from enthusiasm to derision, but nothing stopped him. At the end of the second concert he gave in Lille, he played a rondo of his own composition, which ended in an improvised cadenza. "At the rehearsal he had asked the amateurs who accompanied him to attack the last tutti vigorously, just after the trill which ended the cadenza, adding that he would give the signal by tapping his foot. That evening when it was time for this last piece it was very late and the dilettantes were impatient to go to supper. Since the cadenza, in which as usual Boucher exhibited all his tours de force, seemed as though it would never end, some musicians put their instruments in their cases and quietly left. Their example was so contagious that in a few minutes the whole orchestra had disappeared. Boucher had noticed nothing in the enthusiasm of his playing. He lifted his foot at the start of the trill which ended the cadenza, to attract the attention of the orchestra to the agreed-upon signal. His trill finished, he exulted in the thought of what was coming: the vigorous entry of the orchestra and the applause which would be unleashed by an enthusiastic audience. One can imagine his astonishment when all that came to his ears was the noise made by his own foot. Horrified, he looked around wildly and saw the empty music-stands. But the audience, which was expecting this, broke into a tremendous laugh, and Boucher had no recourse but to join in as best he could."

This long but fragmentary study will perhaps furnish some elements of the natural history of acrobatic virtuosity: it does not concern itself with morality. One can, certainly, deduce that art needs equilibrium, that excess is always a fault, and other elementary truths which the career of Alexander Boucher confirms. But our subject never perceived them. The bitter struggle against a contrary fate never got the better of him. He died on December 27, 1861, at the age of eighty-three, after having played the violin with friends that very day. At his last concert at the Salle Herz in 1859 he appeared to be as full of fire and verve as ever. The last letter we have from him, addressed to Giacomelli on October 1, 1861, is to make a thousand recommendations on the subject of a press release he wanted to review with him and whose text he wanted to perfect: he must have kept a great freshness of spirit to interest himself in these minutiae. Left a widower early, he remarried at sixty-two, choosing a young woman of thirty-one who loved him and whose tenderness did not diminish with the years. She remained vigilant to the point of winning over to the cause of the dead virtuoso a historian, the one we named at the beginning of this essay, and inciting him to a high degree of exaltation.

He is a happy man, after all, who can contemplate the light of day for eighty-three years and die young, who can submit to hard blows without ceasing to believe in the goodness of man, who can nourish the illusion of his genius with such force that he communicates it, even from beyond the grave, to a benevolent censer-bearer.

In juxtaposing two portraits, that of Paganini, riddled with worry and illness, and that of Boucher, alert and defying fate, one may well ask himself which of the two missed out on life.

PAGANINI

If Romanticism, succumbing to the assaults that have not spared it, should one day be scratched from the history of civilization, one can presume that among its last vestiges, among the last names which will still float dimly in our memories, will be that of Niccolò Paganini.

It is not that his works have kept such a power to move us: when one of his pieces is played today, it surely does not produce on the audience the overwhelming impression that his contemporaries experienced. But Paganini's personality projects far beyond his music. One can no longer count the violinists, usually mediocre, who, every five or six years, pride themselves on having discovered the supposed secret of his art; more numerous still are the historians, the romancers, the poets whom Paganini continues to fascinate.

Rather than retrace his agitated life, in which many a period remains obscure in spite of the innumerable accounts that have been written, let us try to reconstruct, through witnesses of the time, the nature of this strange man, at the time when the French public made his acquaintance, in 1831

He was then forty-nine years old, having been born in Genoa in 1782. For two or three years Paris had been waiting for him. Our musicians already knew him by hearsay. In 1805 he had created a sensation at the court, three-quarters French, of Napoleon's sister, the Princess Elisa, at Lucca. Soon after that Boucher de Perthes acclaimed him in a letter written from Leghorn (where the future economist and archeologist was doing a stint as a customs officer): "Paganini is also a Highness in his own field; and when he decides to cut out the clowning and to renounce the honor of being the grand jester of violinists, he will be the Grand Duke, even perhaps the Emperor. . . ."

This reproach of buffoonery seems irreverent to us, but Paganini had recently been severely judged for having played in the church at Lucca a concerto as little religious as possible, to the greater satisfaction of a frivolous public, which was captivated.

It was in 1828 that Parisian music lovers rather suddenly

acquired about our virtuoso a curiosity which continued thereafter to grow. His concert tour in Central Europe had been the
occasion of unprecedented triumphs. In Vienna, in Prague, in
Berlin, he was the recipient of the glory which today sur-
rounds movie stars, boxers, bicycle-racers, and other darlings
of the popular press. The Viennese style in 1828 was "à la
Paganini," even to restaurant menus, snuff boxes, pipes, billiards, canes . . .

At this moment the Paris press entered the game. The young
Revue Musicale, founded by Fétis the preceding year, multiplied its communiqués: "Paganini's first concert in Vienna has
intoxicated the city with an enthusiasm which has not been
seen since." But on the occasion of his sixth concert, we learn
that the enthusiasm has reached its height, that Paganini is "all
the rage," and has dethroned the giraffe recently sent by the
Pasha of Egypt . . . All the seats were sold out in advance
for his concert, all the nobility was there . . . It was thought
that he was leaving for Munich . . . He stayed and gave a
dozen extra concerts . . . He was ill . . . He was going to
come to Paris . . . No, he is in Prague, where he plays, among
other pieces, the *Storm*, a great dramatic sonata with full orchestra, with solos and variations on the fourth string, where
one hears, as in the *Pastoral*, the approach of the storm, the
prayer, the furor of the sea, the hurricane at the height of its
rage, the return to calm, and the explosion of liveliest joy . . .
One follows Paganini to Frankfurt, to Warsaw, to Munich,
where he was invited to play for the queen at the castle of
Tegernsee, and where, at the request of the peasants of the
countryside, he had to play with all the windows wide open
. . . He is leaving for Holland . . . He takes the cure at Bad
Ems . . . , it is not true that he is coming to Paris incog-

nito . . .

Finally on February 26, 1831, the *Revue Musicale* can announce that he is in Paris, that he arrived on the 19th, and that the evening of his arrival he went to applaud la Malibran in *Otello.*

The other reviews form a chorus, the *Courrier des Théâtres,* the *Artiste,* in which a certain Aloysius Block reveals in a "fantasy" entitled *The Two Notes* that at every concert "Paganini plays two shining, cabalistic notes for Satan, who each time deposits them on account in the chancelry of Heaven, against the day of his return to God's grace." More seriously, in the same issue, Fétis concludes a four column article: "What did Paganini lack in order to acquire an indestructible title to renown? To be heard in Paris, in this city of taste and light, where deserved reputations are consolidated, where charlatanism sinks out of sight. At last he is here: the definitive proof is at hand."

And on March 9, at the Opéra, the definitive proof took place, before everyone who counted for anything in Paris. An unheard-of success. We have detailed accounts of this concert. None is as revealing of the spirit of the times as a curious page which falls somewhere between precise reporting and that enormous literature of fantasy which Paganini gave rise to. I extract it from an anonymous story entitled *The Wandering Soul* which appeared in *L'Illustration* a dozen years later, in 1843. The story is told by a soul which has inhabited, among other covers, the body of Paganini; it recounts its tribulations, ending with an episode from the concert at the Opéra:

Over the orchestra, over the parterres, over the boxes, a hushed calm descended; a door at the rear opened, a man appeared:

PAGANINI!

He seemed to glide from behind the door and soon unfolded to view his long supple body, surmounted by that pale face with long flowing black hair, which resembled Christ's, if one did not find in it something of Satan.

He left the back of the stage and advanced, stepping lightly, up to the footlights. His appearance was greeted by a mixture of silent ecstasy and frenetic applause.

He occupied himself at first in making several slow deep bows which were addressed to everyone in such a way that each person thought that they had been meant for him and that he had been singled out with a look.

I, who was behind that look and knew its full import, can tell you how much of his mind and soul Paganini put into it. There was in this look, thrust en masse at all these people, a flamboyant fusion of pride, disdain, genius, shame, scorn, and grandeur. This look said to the audience that they were his slaves, since they had come panting to hear one of his sighs; that they were his tyrants, since they had arrogated to themselves, with a piece of silver, the right to hear him and to judge him . . .

And this look said more: we are two within these walls, myself and you, the people; a man of genius and a crowd without genius; a Paganini who knows that he, alone, is greater than your mass.

This look, full of these thoughts, had nevertheless been so quick that it lasted no more than an instant, and having given the signal to the orchestra, the artist raised his bow on high and let it fall violently on his violin, as if he were giving it a hatchet blow.

Then all was begun, not his beautiful melody, but his playing, the concert, the great struggle; for in those first moments he sawed rudely on the strings with the harsh horsehairs of the bow, and the instrument gave forth mournful, piercing, furious sounds, as those of the lion who wakes up angry, and roars . . .

The musicians had the written score in front of them, Paganini's score, and he, although he had neither music stand nor paper before his eyes, he played with no hesitation what he had composed, which responded to the orchestra score, and nevertheless, there was something so spontaneous, so fiery in his playing, that I can not understand how it could be cold memory that furnished him with such inspirations.

The orchestra was as excited and trembling as the slave before its master.

The public was in ecstasy: it was caught up in Paganini's genius, which became, one might almost say, incarnate in each one of them; they all felt their hearts dilate and melt in delicious emotions, when the bow, balanced lightly on the strings, made them quiver with love, made them palpitate with pleasure; or, on the contrary, when it expressed the fury of war or the rage of the tempest, then one saw their faces contract, the eyebrows drawn in a frown, the teeth grind and gnash, and heavy sighs escape sorrowfully from each breast, as if there was in all the hall but one soul, one single thing: the violin.

Meanwhile Paganini, who had withdrawn into himself, into an interior world of his own, no longer saw the crowd, only his violin, his beloved violin. He enveloped it with his eyes, with his arms, he pressed it to his hollow cheek, he clasped it to his breast, he inhaled its sounds and breathed with it; he no doubt saw the sounds escaping like flashes of lightning, for his burning eyes, fixed on the strings, which he seemed to oppress with his look, followed them. Never were love's embraces more passionate, nor had deeper looks been found in adoring eyes.

And his bow, like an angel's sword, shot forth flames and rays from this prodigious instrument; it threw off incandescent harmonies, it dispensed sweet melodies like the perfumes of the Orient, it let loose resounding thunderclaps like those of God. And other times, when, after having whipped it violently, the great artist put down his bow, there was still a new sound, very thin and frail, which his left hand made by plucking the strings, and which rapidly died away, like the sparks given off by electricity.

After this first piece, Paganini, resuming his gracious smile and making the same deep bow, retired in the midst of thunderous applause and shouts.

He returned, and acclamations were again hurled through the air, to thank him for what he had done, to applaud what he would do, to render homage to him simply because he was Paganini.

This time his mind ordered three strings to be silent, leaving only that good silver string which you know. He said nothing, but one knew that he was going to play the variations on the march from *Mosè*.

Sublime musician, why do you suppress those strings? Why do you deny yourself those heavenly effects you introduced to this world when, sounding all the strings at once, you produced, by yourself alone, a concert of harmony in which each string was called on at the same time? Who forces you to impose this martyrdom, to restrict yourself this way? Why this whim, man of genius?

No, it is not a whim, nor merely a prodigious feat; it is a lesson; it is to reveal to men what is hidden in a single string, and how by striking it with the bow there will flow from it the most incomprehensible treasure of music. Thus Moses struck the rock, and the rock poured forth its waters; Paganini touches the silver string, and there wells up an infinite series of sounds and melodies.

He has taught his violin and all the world what is meant by "harmonic sound."

When Paganini has on this single string run through the gamut of sounds, and as he nears the approach to the bridge, one cries out like God to the sea: "This far, but no further," Paganini retraces his steps and begins again, and already he has gone farther, for the harmony gives him other vibrations, lifts him to other realms, where he drinks abundantly and without end.

And this sound that he finds in another universe could not in reality have come from ours; it has an indefinable limpidity, an exquisite sweetness, an ethereal tenuousness, a mysterious brilliance, so that one wonders whether to call it a sound, a light, or a perfume . . .

Paganini appeared a third time, this time to take up all four strings with renewed passion. No more soft delights, no more celestial raptures; now it is the Ocean which rolls and heaves tempestuously; now it is the creation of the earth or its frightful upheavals, the volcano which erupts and spews out the flaming entrails of the earth; here are the last convulsions of the universe when Jehovah will stop it in its path and say to it: "Die!" Paganini does not mean to paint any of this, but these things must be summoned to mind in order to understand his marvelous fury when he brandishes his bow to arrive at the grandiose, the terrible.

Then all the strings quivered at one time, shrieked under the redoubled blows of his fingers, which fell like the hail that accompanies thunder and lightning. The bow, for its part, tore at them, stung them, gouged them, flayed them alive, trampled them savagely; they cried out in pain . . . and all the cries were sublime.

And Paganini, in his genius and his passion, savored these wounds; he roared and struggled in this martyrdom of the violin; he pressed it harder and harder, he struck it, he bruised it, he inflamed it in its agonies . . . and this savagery was sublime.

And the orchestra, as with one body, panting, frightened, followed with horror the bow of the maestro . . . and this horror was sublime.

And the people, the crowd, hung on his bow, were exalted, ravished by terror, bruised with emotion, overcome with enthusiasm, unable to breathe . . . and this effect was sublime.

And the concert was over . . .

Despite the spellbinding talent of present-day virtuosos, we shall not meet again, in the twentieth century, the satanic emotions of that audience of 1831. This is undoubtedly because technique has progressed since then and put Paganinian prowess within the reach of numerous violinists. Without speaking of those artists of world renown such as Kubelik,

Heifetz, Milstein, Stern, Francescatti, Szeryng, and Oistrakh, many lesser artists have accustomed us to prodigious feats on the violin. But above all the atmosphere has changed. Not one of them trails after him so many legends, so many true stories, quarrels with kings, princesses swooning on hearing him, fantastic recipes for success, Stradivarii received as gifts—and none of them is afflicted with a physique capable of attracting attention so imperiously. "He is as thin as one can be," writes his biographer Schottky, an observer on the whole sympathetic, "with a sallow skin, the nose of an eagle pointing ahead, and long bony fingers. He seems hardly able to hold up his clothes, and when he makes a bow, his body moves in such a singular fashion that one fears at any moment that one might see his feet separate from his body, and the whole man collapse in a pile of bones." A physician, Dr. Bennati, studied him and described him in a more objective way:

Although he is only forty-seven years old [he was in reality forty-nine at the time], his extreme thinness and his lack of teeth, by retracting his mouth and making his chin more salient, give his face the expression of an older man. The large head, supported on a long thin neck, offers at first sight a rather striking disproportion with his spindly limbs; a high forehead, wide and square, an aquiline nose strongly chiselled, brows perfectly arched, a mouth full of wit and cunning, recalling a little that of Voltaire, rather large flaring ears, long black hair falling loosely to his shoulders and contrasting with his pale complexion, all give to Paganini a physiognomy which is out of the ordinary and which represents to a certain degree the originality of his genius.

It has been wrongly said that an expression of physical pain gave Paganini's features a wild aspect of melancholy that sprang from a profound disillusion with life. I avow that a long acquaintance with Paganini has never given me such an idea of his character; I have always found him gay, witty, ready to laugh, even with his friends, entering into children's games with his charming little Achilles; and I can speak of Paganini better than anyone. One notices in him the "extensibility" of the capsular ligaments of the shoulders, the relaxed state of the ligaments which join the hand and the forearm, the carpus and the metacarpus, and the phalanxes to each other. The hand is no larger than it should be; but it is doubled in reach by the extensibility of all the parts. Thus, for example, he imparts to the first phalanxes of the left hand which touch the strings a movement of extraordinary flexion, which takes them in a lateral direction to their natural flexion without changing the position of his hand, and all this done with facility, precision, and speed. His auditory sense is well developed; he hears what is said, even in a low voice, at a great distance, and his eardrum is so sensitive that he experiences real pain when one speaks in a loud voice near him, and from the side. In the midst of the deafening noise of the percussion instruments of a large orchestra, he needs only a light touch of the finger to tune his violin; he can tell equally well, in the same circumstances, if even the softest instrument is out of tune, and this at an incredible distance. On several occasions he has shown the perfection of his musical organ by playing on pitch on a violin which was out of tune.

Paganini is steeped in music; we are told that at the age of five, the ringing of the church bells in his native town in Italy produced sometimes a great joy, sometimes a strange melancholy; he could not listen to the sound of the church organ without being moved to tears. Even when he is weak and ill, the first stroke of the bow is like an electric spark which comes to give him new life, all his nerves vibrate like the strings of his violin, and his brain has no other faculty but the expression of the transports of his musical soul; he and his instrument are one . . .

Such is the man who inflamed the imagination of the Romantic world. The infatuation of the French yielded in no respect to that of the Viennese. The poets rushed in. The *Almanach des Muses* published an invocation on *Paganini's Name* signed by Mme. Marceline Valmore, who, trying for too easy a play on words, fell into a distracted lyricism.

> Paganini! sweet name which beats on my memory,
> And like an angel's wing, awakes my heart,
>   Sweet name which weeps, which cries out: Glory!
>   Plucked from the celestial choir!
> All heaven's kisses are in your harmony;
> Sweet name, lovely halo lighting his genius,
> You ring with music, attached to his rounds;
> He drags you before the idolatrous crowd;
> The whole earth is your theater,
> You are called his soul; You will live forever.
> Yes, from a different spark this soul was formed,
> Yes, God gave it life, it was his well-beloved;
> Yes, a thousand love-birds murmur in his breast;
> Their sighs escape them, they sing under his hand;
>   And in these soft sighings
>   Which rustle like flowers,
>   There is balm for every hurt,
>   And tears for all laments!
> O! what rapture, what bliss, what joy,
> When such a song takes wings!
> The soul has no shelter
> It fears to leave, it flies back to him.
>   God, protect in its travels
>   The living echo of your voice,
>   Which suspends the roar of the storm
>   Or makes it moan under his fingers;
>   Bar the sorrowful paths
>   To this wandering melody,
>   For his sublime malady
>   Cures many a sad heart!

It is true that an adverse faction made itself heard. One finds, here and there, some who carp, like the author of this anonymous quatrain:

> This virtuoso inimitable,
> If he were kind, generous, and sincere,
> If he changed his ways and combed his hair,
> Would be a man incomparable.

A. M. Poupin, publishing in 1836 his *Etudes phrénologiques* (*Phrenological Studies*), brands him as the prototype of the miser, "the sly, bad, rich man who holds our good French coins so cheap; Paganini, the ungrateful artist, who by a few strokes of the bow, has carried off twenty trunks of our gold, without letting one small portion fall on our poor people . . ." The avarice of Paganini! There is an enigma that will not be soon resolved. We will read a little later some of the jibes to which it gave rise. How can one reconcile them with the royal present of 20,000 gold francs which Paganini made to Berlioz in 1837?

Even supposing that this gift was made with the intention of refuting the accusation of parsimony and to conciliate himself with the Paris press and the public, as has been said, Paganini had made, in other circumstances, disinterested gestures. J.-G. Prod'homme has cited more than one example. But it is certain that in everyday life, our man kept his accounts with a rigor that was ill-suited to his earnings, and still less to the idea that the Romantics had formed of the artist, a demi-god soaring above everyday realities and notoriously incapable of doing a sum. In any case, his miserliness, real or pretended, continually excited the spleen of innumerable gazetteers, before and—still more—after his death, which took

place, as we know, on May 27, 1840. This is what we find
printed (without the name of the author) less than six weeks
later, on July 5, in the *Ménestrel:*

Long live death, for that is where you learn the truth about yourself! Here is what is related about the virtuoso whose violin will
weep forever: Paganini's will is a curious thing. Out of an estate of
several million francs, the great artist leaves to his mother a pension
of only 2000 francs for life. No one knows the extent of the
avarice of Paganini, who amassed so much gold and built marble
palaces with the fourth string of his violin. There was no ingenious ruse that he did not invent in order to economize. To
understand it, one should have seen him travel as we have seen
him, nimbly climbing up on the seat of the diligence—he, a
millionaire. When the coach stopped for dinner, and his companions said to him, "Well, aren't you coming to eat?" he replied
in those wonderful words that even Harpagon had not thought
of, "I'm not hungry three francs worth!" Isn't that as good as
anything in antiquity? And Paganini, after having totted up the
account of his appetite, stayed in the coach and devoured a
Spartan repast of bread and cheese. Two years ago he went to
Marseilles to breathe the warm air; he had then fallen into that
regime of atmospheric medicine, the last word of science when
all hope is lost, the last resource of the Medical School, which,
having used all the classic methods and all the boldest experiments,
sends you to die in the sun. At Marseilles Paganini met a young
amateur enamored of his talent and took advantage of him. With
the nonchalance of genius the illustrious artist established himself
in the young man's home; he took an apartment in his house, a
place at his table, he called him friend and said to him: "Lodge me,
feed me, let me die here at your side, and I will leave you my
secret and my violin." The young man at first was very well satisfied with the bargain, but soon he found that the charges of
hospitality were heavy. Paganini said to him in a mournful voice:

"Alas, we have not long to be together!" Then he played the sick man, he played the dying man, and he lived that way for eighteen months at the expense of his young friend. He would have stayed there till the end, if the doctors had not obliged him to go breathe the air of Nice. After the death of the great artist, the young man waited confidently for the result of a promise for which he had paid dearly; but Paganini had other things than gratitude in his head! He took with him into the tomb the secret which he could not pass on, and he left his violin to the entire artistic world, which is already fighting over it at the auction house. Sovereigns have sent ambassadors to buy this famous violin which carries with it so many legends. There is not a virtuoso who does not hope to double his price by means of this magic instrument. So it will go high. But would not the purchaser do better to keep this violin by putting it in Paganini's mausoleum?

But there is not just *one* enigma in connection with Paganini. One could name a number of them: that of his technique, that of his fortune, about which there have been some amazing guesses, that of his character, jovial according to some, irascible according to most observers; Berlioz saw him break a mirror in anger in the foyer of the theater in Marseilles on hearing that the hall was almost empty, but Dr. Bennati has shown us a Paganini "gay, witty, laughing, even with his friends," and his correspondence confirms this. There is still the enigma of his illness, of his death, prematurely announced, and when it finally came, so mysterious that after five exhumations of the poor corpse, uncertainties still remain.

Marginal to the accounts that were written about these macabre events, is this one, published in 1843 in *France musicale* under the fanciful signature of "Paul de Kick" (an evident allusion to Paul de Kock), and written in a style that is still used by some of the powerful weeklies today. It reports, with a certain accent of truth, the reactions of the inhabitants of Nice to the news of Paganini's death:

The streets of Nice were filled with sun, movement, noise; joy, sorrow, and idleness that all mingled together; having noticed that people were stopping before one of the houses of the Rue du Gouvernement, and that a crowd was forming fast, I took myself in that direction. Officers and policemen soon made part of the crowd; people arrived from all sides, pushed each other, questioned each other.

"What's going on?"

"It's nothing," says one.

"It's a fire!" cries another.

"What's that?" interrupts a third, becoming alarmed.

"Oh, no," says a shopkeeper, shrugging his shoulders, "It's nothing . . . Paganini is dead!"

Then the tumult breaks out. Each one laughs at the haste with which he had come running, and stops the newcomers to repeat, "It's nothing . . . Paganini is dead!"

The gossips, disappointed, make a panegyric to the deceased after their fashion. One says he was a miser and refused to give a concert for the poor. Another adds that he had been in the galleys and had learned to play the violin there. A third says with emphasis that he had great talent, but that the strings of his instrument were made from the intestines of his wife . . . and a thousand other absurdities.

Tired of such litanies, I took leave of these fishwives and entered the narrow alley where Paganini had lived. As I mounted the stair, I met a rather well-dressed girl, who was weeping, although she carried a purse in her hand. I asked her the reason for her tears.

She replied that her master, M. Paganini, had just died and that she would be without a place.

"And where did he live, may I ask?"

"Here . . . go on in."

Curiosity propelled me into his apartment. The celebrated violinist whom I had applauded with ecstasy, and who had had need of nothing less than his immense talent to contain the laughter that his bizarre person had excited, lay there on his bed, with a napkin in front of him, on which could be seen the remains of a pigeon.

The servant told me: "The poor man seemed to know that he would not finish that pigeon . . . He said to me, yesterday when he gave me the money to buy two pounds of beef: 'Zulietta, I should dearly like to eat some pigeon!' 'Well, sir, then give me twelve sous more.' 'Twelve sous!' he said, making a worse face than usual, 'twelve sous, oh, that's too dear, Zulietta! . . . And yet,' he added with a sigh, 'I really would like some, Zulietta! Try at least, my dear, to find one for eight sous; for you see, my child, there are so many bones in those terrible pigeons . . . it's not solid meat like the big piece of beef you buy!' So you see a little what it's like, sir! . . . Here is the poor man who is said to be richer than Croesus . . . he bought sou by sou . . . He was hardly dead when his son, whom you heard weeping in the next room, gave me this purse . . . If he keeps it up, he'll go through his good father's money!"

However my eyes remained fixed on the dead body of Paganini, whose face, dry like his violin, had, in spite of its ugliness, the solemn cast which death lays on its works. I could hear a coming and going in the room, but I saw nothing but Paganini and his silent violin which hung on the wall.

I do not know what bizarre ideas passed through my mind . . . it was not only one death I saw . . . but two! . . . Paganini . . . and his Stradivarius! . . whose silence seemed to me no less imposing.

I recalled its accents, its modulations expressing life in all its tones and filling thousands of listeners with a delirious agitation.

This instrument is dead, I said to myself . . . dead with Paganini!
. . . A single soul animated both of them!— And almost in spite
of myself, my eyes went alternately from the purple lips, the
glassy eyes, the leathery face of the one to the slack strings, the
disheveled bow, the dusty sides, empty of sound, of the other.

Some old women, more out of charity than the hope of a
recompense, shrouded the dead millionaire; seeing this, I wished,
for my part, to perform the last rites for the poor violin. I spread
a white cloth on a console table; I gently laid on it the body of
the violin; but, by accident, having hit the corner of the marble
table, the instrument gave a feeble sound which made me start, as
if I had heard, all of a sudden, a sound emanate from the livid
mouth of Paganini. I looked at it one last time before covering it,
and having placed a crown of everlasting at one end and two
lighted tapers at the other, I slowly crossed the chamber to go out.

Turning, I saw in the corner a young officer hastily sketching
the dead man, while two urchins stuck their heads through the
half-open door and with bright eyes were peering under the cur-
tains where Paganini lay.

Marlborough, after his death, was interred, as we learn from the
song. It is not the same with Paganini, for he was embalmed according to the new procedure.— The religious authorities deny
him a bit of ground to be buried in, because he died without the
sacraments. The steamboat refuses to receive him on board as a
passenger to be transported to his native city, Genoa. The pro-
prietor of the house wants to rent his apartment. What will be
done with this poor millionaire? He is being put in a vault, awaiting something better.

May God take the soul of this great artist, because the people
of Nice do not want his body!

This shabby piece of journalism seems to me to merit re-
production, in that it sums up rather well the conflicting
opinions Paganini left behind him, the slurs that followed him

beyond the grave, the admiration that his genius continued to
inspire and in which there persisted a strange impression of
the supernatural. This impression is none other, I think, than
that aroused by a certain personal magnetism, that hypnotic
power possessed to some degree by all the great performers and
that could well be the most typical attribute of the born
virtuoso.

There is something which shows us, more clearly than does
backstairs journalism, Paganini in the grip of those problems
that created his fame, his fortune, and his very real bitterness
in defending it.

A happy chance makes me the possessor of a manuscript
from his hand, the first page of a melody entitled *la Farfaletta,
canzoncina con accompagnamento di Piano-forte*. It would be
of slight interest if it were not enriched with this dedication:

Questo sgorbio è fatto ed offerto all' egregia Virtuosa Chiare
Loveday non solamente in segno d'ammirazione del suo splen-
dentissimo talento anzi come pruova di generosa amicizia per
l'amabile suonatrice.

                    Il signor Barone Niccolò Paganini
                    Nell' Albergo di Neothermes
                    Via della Vittoria 16 Giugno 1838.
(This scribble is made and offered to the remarkable virtuoso
Clara Loveday, not only as a sign of admiration for her most
splendid talent but also as a proof of my warm friendship for
the amiable pianist.)

Now, on this same June 16, 1838, Paganini addressed the
following letter to the father of the "remarkable virtuoso,"

Douglas Loveday, an English lawyer who had settled in Paris, and who had lodged him and his son Achilles for four months.

Monsieur,

I am forced to express to you my surprise on seeing how little thought you have taken toward remitting the debt you owe me. This negligence on your part forces me to refresh your memory of circumstances which you should not have forgotten.

I present you with my little account in the hope that you will pay it as soon as possible.

For having given twelve lessons to Mademoiselle your daughter to make her understand the manner in which she should express the music and the sense of the notes which she played in my presence: 2,400 francs.

For having myself played in your house on eight different occasions several pieces of music: 24,000 francs. Total: 26,400 francs.

I do not add to this account all the lessons which I gave *verbally* to Mademoiselle your daughter while I was at your table, all the while paying my expenses down to the last centime, wishing to make a present of the trouble I took at those times, as I tried to give her the correct ideas of musical knowledge, desiring that she grasp them and profit from them.

I shall not add another word to make you aware that it is proper to pay people who render services to you and lend you their efforts, since you have not failed to tell me your opinion on this point in giving me your advice in the affair of Dr. Cr . . . io, in which you judged it incumbent on me to pay 110 francs for having received, happily for my health, some counsels that were given me by chance at your house. You will understand, Monsieur, that there is too great a difference between the so-called visits of this Doctor and my lessons, and especially my sessions of playing, not to realize that in proportion, I am much more modest in my demands than he is in his.

I pray you, then, to acquit yourself at once of this debt that you owe me, for I warn you that in the contrary event, I shall not fail to follow the example that others give me, being persuaded that I have, at least, the same right.

I salute you most distinctly, and have the honor of being,

NICCOLÒ PAGANINI

At the bottom of the facsimile of this letter, which is, apart from the signature, in the hand of Paganini's son, there is this note by Loveday:

The letter of which the above is a copy is to be found at Mr. Loveday's, 40 Rue St. Lazare, waiting to be deposited in a Museum or Archives of "extraordinary men."

A week later, on June 24, the *Revue et Gazette musicale de Paris* published the following letter, preceded by this heading:

A LETTER ATTRIBUTED TO PAGANINI

There has been circulating in Paris for several days a letter from Paganini addressed to Mr. Loveday, which we are far from believing to be authentic, as the subject and the expressions are strange; nevertheless, as the best way to stop its effect is to furnish the celebrated virtuoso an occasion of denying it publicly, we are going to bring it *textually* to the eyes of our readers so that they may, while awaiting the reply of the great artist to whom it is attributed, appreciate all the impropriety of what we regard as a mystification.

The letter in question followed.

But meanwhile, on June 17, Loveday had addressed one to Paganini, so long that I shall reproduce *in extenso* only about the first third:

Monsieur le baron,

I adhere to the principles which I had the honor to express to
you when you consulted me, nine days ago, on your latest
difficulty, to wit: whether you should pay the bill of Dr. Crosiero,
the distinguished doctor whom you engaged to care for you after
the retirement of Dr. Majendie, who had until then been your
physician. Truth is an essence which never changes. It is always
the same.

You have lived with me for ninety-nine days, you and your son.
I am proud to say that I and all my family took extreme care to
please you, to render you all possible services. In my capacity as a
physician, I am intensely persuaded that I have had, on several
occasions, the happiness of saving your life: since I do not profess
Medicine, I do not ask you anything for my services of this nature;
as your secretary, I ask nothing either. But in my capacity as
Jurisconsult and Lawyer, the numerous consultations which I had
with you in relation to certain disastrous steps which you had
contemplated and from which, by my counsels, I deterred you,
form an article important enough to merit your attention. In
England, I should have presented a bill for a sum which would
have given a severe jolt to your fortune, colossal as it is. Here I
shall content myself with claiming as honorarium the modest sum
of 18,000 francs; but I shall prove if need be that at 25,000 francs
you will not be paying for half the services I rendered you. If I
wanted to put a price only on the services I did you in relation to
the Casino Paganini, I could prove that my advice was worth more
than 140,000 francs to you. And then, your projected trip to Saint
Petersburg, as well as that to New York; and again that tiresome
correspondence I maintained for you . . . I hardly know how
you could repay me . . . !

I disregard all the advice of a medical nature which I have
given you, even when, after tiring disputes, I prevailed on you to
abstain from following the prescription of the beautiful somnam-
bulist, which, if you had followed it, O, misery! (I have confirmed the fact from Messrs Cap and Planche) would have burned

you from the skin of the lower belly to the dorsal spine . . .
bowels and all. There would not have been enough left to make
an E string for your famous Guarnerius!

But medicine, as I have said, is not my profession; I do not ask
anything for it. I love music, I appreciate your admirable talent.
But my profession is that of Jurisconsult and Lawyer. I have
served you faithfully, honorably, conscientiously in these capac-
ities; and God knows (parenthetically) if you love quibbling,
and yet you have not thought of offering me any compensation
beyond a pinch of snuff, which I always returned with interest,
except the promise of a snuffbox of . . . wood, which you have
not yet sent."

There follows a detailed account of the lessons which Loveday had given to the young Achilles: ninety-nine days of
lessons at 200 francs a day, or a total of 19,800 francs, which
were added to his honorarium as a jurist (18,000 francs). He
proposes to have recourse to a semi-official arbitration to avoid
the expenses of a lawsuit, and after other recriminations presented in an ironic vein, he closes with this salutation:

In conclusion if (as you write me, you have the honor to be
Niccolò Paganini) I, for my part, have the advantage of not being
he, and independent of that I have the honor of being
your very humble servant,
DOUGLAS LOVEDAY.

Upon which, on July 24, in the same *Revue et Gazette
musicale de Paris*, there appeared this new letter from Paganini:

Monsieur,
A certain Mr. Douglas Loveday published in the *Gazette
musicale* a letter which I had addressed to him, about a month

ago, and took care to speak of the answer he made me. Desiring in my turn to publish some observations on this reply, I ask you, monsieur, to be good enough to insert them in your honorable journal.

Accept, monsieur, the expression of my most distinguished sentiments.

NICCOLÒ PAGANINI.

To Mr. Douglas Loveday.

Monsieur,

It pleased you some time ago to publish a letter which you took seriously and which I had addressed to you with the sole object of proving how easy it is to quarrel with someone when the fancy takes us. My letter was merely a humorous revenge for the bill which you set up to the profit of your friend Mr. Cr . . . o, a distinguished physician, as you say. In effect, having decided to help him earn money at any cost, you were clever enough to metamorphose into visits at ten francs some how-do-you-dos that your friend, the celebrated physician, addressed to me in greeting me when I lived in your house, politenesses, that, for the rest, I hastened to put a stop to in barring the door of my apartment to the celebrated doctor, as soon as I saw that the salutations were becoming serious, and that he was preparing to reinforce them with orders, of which, for the good of my health, I doubted the efficacy.

What did I do to answer you? I presented in my turn a bill of 27,400 francs for lessons, musical sessions, etc., given to Mlle. your daughter. It was an apothecary's bill in return for a doctor's bill. We should have been quits; but not at all. You took fright, you thought you saw in my letter an intention of extracting money, a demand. Perhaps you had visions of bailiffs and their staves, and you ran to put yourself under the protection of public opinion by giving my letter to the papers and passing it off as an act of desperation on my part and consequently a masterpiece of avarice.

You played a good game. But what proves to me that you were not joking and that your intention was not to amuse the public at our expense, is that at the same time you gave my letter to the papers, you did not give them the one you wrote in reply, demanding 37,800 francs from me for a debt that you hastened to fabricate, to counterbalance my pretended claim.

Paganini continued the discussion and ended with this stinging barb aimed at Clara Loveday:

Finally I question that the lessons for Mlle. your daughter could be worth 200 francs apiece, for, as far as I can tell, Mlle. your daughter lacks that faculty by which the soul of an interpreter passes to the tips of his fingers to translate sounds into emotions. In spite of all the pains the good young lady has gone to, goes to, and will go to, she will never succeed in having the right touch. Therefore she will find it difficult to give lessons at 200 francs each. I think she will have greater success if she gives herself over to the pantomime for which she seemed to have a great inclination, during all the time I saw her play . . .

This ironic appreciation of Clara Loveday's talents is hard to reconcile with the dedication we have reproduced. It is also contradicted by numerous reviews of concerts that appeared in the journals of the time, from the pens of musicians as well qualified as Elwart, Henri Montan-Berton, and others . . . We remark also that on November 25, 1837, at the inauguration of the *Casino Paganini*, that enterprise launched by speculators to exploit the name of the illustrious son of Genoa, with his support and financial backing (the affair turned out badly, but that is not the question), Clara Loveday appeared with great success as soloist in the "Piece for Salon by Weber," and although Paganini did not play, he stood security to some extent by appearing for a moment in the hall.

In all probability Paganini vented on Clara the anger that her father had provoked in him, not without reason, it would seem. For the lawyer must have been excitable as well as verbose, as will be seen from a pamphlet twenty pages long, dated December 28, 1821, whose title page gives the tone:

Petition to the Chamber of Deputies, on behalf of Mr. Douglas Loveday, Englishman and Protestant; complaining of the seduction worked on his two daughters and his niece, in a house of instruction in which he had placed them in Paris, and where the credulity of these young persons was abused with the aid of superstitious terrors, obsessions and false miracles, to convert them suddenly to Catholicism, in the absence, without the knowledge of, and against the wishes of their parents.

And I shall cite the peroration, not that it has the slightest connection with Paganini and his apothecary's bills: it is too pretty a model of the style of the times at the dawn of Romanticism for me to deprive my reader:

Deputies of France! I have seen my daughter torn from my arms, her natural sentiments strangled in her soul; the sacred weapon of religion turned against me; the authority which should protect me, silent in my defense; for a moment I said to myself: "There is no succor for an outraged father in this nation which prides itself on its hospitality"; but I turned my attentions toward its representatives, and I have kept up hope . . .

VII

On Criticism

IN AN INTERESTING and closely reasoned reply to an inquiry opened by the magazine *Arts* on the present confusion in musical tendencies, Jean Martinon takes into account, as he should, the responsibilities of the critic. When he states our insufficiencies in measured terms, we are with him at heart. We do not deny that the profession suffers both from its heterogeneous makeup and from the vagueness of its doctrine. The critical fraternity consists, by and large, of two groups: composers and non-composers, the latter more inclined to err in matters of technique; the former exposed to painful conflicts between their esthetic credo and the exigencies of their career. As to doctrine, after a good number of serious books (running, that is, to 300 or more pages each) and several thousand articles, it has not yet been decided if music criticism should be subjective, objective, or in between.

Jean Martinon has therefore the best reasons for desiring improvement; but he must allow me to differ with him in the direction to follow.

His wish, resolutely optimistic, would be to see us devote ourselves exclusively to the exaltation of the beautiful and to grant only silence and scorn to the rest, which, according to him, would die of itself.

If only that were true! If this self-destruction of all ugliness were really the order of things, what a marvelous profession ours would be! When one has grown bald with the years, and, tired of the storms of life, aspires to nothing more than a universal serenity, it would be a singular relief to break contact with all that is base, degrading, or simply mediocre, in order to devote oneself to the contemplation of the lofty heights. The young would perhaps find this pastime a little static. I cannot recall without shame the impure pleasure I took, in the old days, in making a game of massacring certain innocent categories of art. Times have changed, I feel as conciliatory and kind as a venerable professor.

However, I do not think that the expression of our enthusiasm in the presence of a work of art serves it well unless a simultaneous, or previous, action of clearing the rubbish has assured it a field in which to breathe and grow: the gardener does not expect flowers in weed-infested ground.

Eliminating the shoddy is a negative duty, but a necessary one, for the simple reason that what the shoddy drains away in attendance, in receipts, in success, is taken from works of quality. There is no great originality in saying that the most interesting part of a concert audience is often the least well-to-do, because (no, there is no hidden political thought here) in the inexpensive seats there are no complimentary tickets or season subscriptions bought for reasons of family tradition. There one finds only those who are thirsty for music. The badge of a real passion for music is a seat in the top balcony, dark, steep, and badly ventilated as it is in the older concert halls.

Now, if this clientele with a limited budget is led astray by astute advertising to a recital given by a second-rate imitator of Horowitz or a gutter Paganini, there goes the money it might have spent the next day to hear a musician of merit. It is as stupid as that; but it necessitates a prophylaxis that could well be our major service.

In the appreciation of new works, the very fact that there is a diversity of tastes often imposes on the critic a wise reserve. For us to grasp, on the first hearing, the essence of a composition of radically new technique, there must exist a pre-established harmony between the composer's sensibility and our own. This is not always the case. Certain music, whose beauty we sense, discloses itself only slowly, while other works exercise too soon an attraction which quickly fades. Here we find ourselves in agreement with Jean Martinon. To point out what seems to us to possess real character, even if the technique is uneven or gauche, should be our primary task. Only what is false or platitudinous should be challenged.

In the case of performers, for the reasons cited above, the duty of discriminating becomes our first charge; and we should expect to find ourselves alone, against the current, in uncomfortable situations.

For the fluctuations of success obey laws we cannot comprehend. At his last appearance, Ysaÿe, past his peak, it is true, but rich with a great past, played before a handful of faithful friends, lost in the immense Opéra. Kubelik, old and having lost that transcendent technique which had been his glory, continued to fill the same hall, because of the speed with which he could play. Others, who were born and remain mediocre, stay in the limelight for several seasons, relying on clever strategy, perseverance, a good impresario, friends in high places, and an iron nerve.

In such cases, criticism has a word to say.

With what result? Will its flute-like voice be heard over the din of the brasses of publicity? Will it send one more listener to the little-known genius or the beginner who is trying for his big chance? Will it turn one way from the charlatan who has arrived?

A rich subject of inquiry—but, to safeguard any good opinion that we may have of ourselves, just the type of inquiry to avoid.

Ten years after Jean Martinon took his stand, an article by Mr. Armand Machabey (*Musica*, December 1954) reopened the old case against music criticism. *Critique musicale quotidienne* (*Music Criticism in the Daily Press*) says the title: actually it concerns French music criticism, for the study in question takes its examples only from the newspapers of Paris. It is in two parts; the first demolishes, the second seeks to reconstruct.

We shall not linger over the first. Similar diatribes have been launched many times by composers who had a grievance against the critical fraternity, or by critics momentarily unemployed. Those whom heaven endowed with a light pen have been able to lend charm to this exercise, and by citing ridiculous and contradictory judgments, put the amused reader on their side. Mr. Machabey is content to exhume four citations which have already seen much service. I permit myself to recommend to him the arsenal, all prepared and flaming new, which the *Lexicon of Musical Invective* compiled by Nicolas Slonimsky puts at his disposal. Also, since he makes a great case for intellectual probity, denied, it would seem, to most of the "journalists," he should refrain from reserving his blows for puppets who are only too vulnerable, while eschewing the more substantial targets. In this article and in his copious *Traité de la Critique musicale* (*Treatise on Music Criticism*), where he denounces still more vigorously the decadence of French criticism after Berlioz, we search in vain for the names of Gaston Carraud, of Laloy, of Marnold, who, around 1900, brought to Debussy, to Fauré, to Ravel something other than "condemnations without appeal, formulated with violence, bitterness, irony, or ignorance." Still more shocking is the omission of the name of Paul Dukas, such a penetrating and admirably informed critic, and although in the trade himself, so fair-minded—this, on the part of a theoretician who denies the faculty of impartiality to all composers.

Let us pass on, and turn our attention to the remedies Mr. Machabey proposes.

He has suggested one unwittingly, when in the treatise mentioned above, he expressed the regret that "the historians hold aloof, or are held aloof, from day-to-day criticism." More postively, his article in *Musica* gives us a glimpse of a salvation to be achieved through a specialized study, a Course in Music Criticism, like the one created twenty years ago at the Moscow Conservatory. In fact, this course proved to have a blinding efficiency. It was started in 1934: two years later, Moscow possessed a critical bloc homogeneous enough to hurl itself in a body, one fine day in 1936, against the unfortunate Shostakovitch, the genius of the previous hour.

Not counting its bellicose activities, the task of criticism consists essentially, according to Mr. Machabey, in classifying works and artists by means of a system of references borrowed from the past: only posterity is in a position to determine the real value of a work. Its verdict will be known by adopting the sociological unit of the "century." If, in a hundred years' time, posterity accepts a work, "it is because it had hidden within it a polyvalence far surpassing its original value."

So be it. But what worthy exceptions when we stop to think! Who cared about Pérotin the Great, a century after his death? And Guillaume de Machaut, and all the polyphonists of the Renaissance? How many great Italians have seen the light of day again after a neglect of two or three centuries? Let us accept, however, the unit of time set by Mr. Machabey. It gives us that "fundamental indication" that, for a period of one hundred years "three per cent at most of the works played have survived up to our time . . . Thus, each time a critic affirms that this or that concerto, this new symphony is a masterpiece, he has ninety-seven chances of being wrong, and only three of hitting it right; the proportion is inverted if he attacks the score . . ."

It would be too easy to retort that, not being impregnated with the strong discipline of a "school of Moscow," the judgment of the critics, in the presence of the same work, rarely agrees, which should bring the percentages to more modest levels. And when that does not happen, what difference would it make! It so happens that Mr. Machabey has occasionally reviewed concerts himself. I have read his columns. They have covered a Mozart concert, a performance of the Ninth Symphony by Mengelberg, some military marches by Klamberg, and other similar subjects which do not require either the mobilization of a laborious system of references, or the unfolding of any very complex mental operations. And it does not appear that they will greatly preoccupy the music lovers of the year 2040 and beyond. Neither in their aim nor their content nor their style do they differ much from those signed by the music critics of the Paris press, even those who pride themselves the least on dogmatizing and prophesying.

For the rest, I should not like to compromise anyone, but I think I can say that most of us do not believe we are called upon to classify performers and composers, or to "formulate a judgment on the destiny of a score" in future centuries. We know, and the reading of Mr. Machabey's treatise can only confirm this, that no criterion has been found that is valid for all times and all countries. Our readers know as well that if by chance a critic hazards a prophecy, nothing should be seen in it but a more forceful way of expressing a liking or an aversion of the moment. If, in cold blood, and for eternity, the critic pretended to the double role of the marker in the *Meistersinger* and extra-lucid clairvoyant, he would soon be preaching in the desert, for something else entirely is expected from him.

The major attraction of our profession, as I have already had occasion to say, is the feeling that we can sometimes create in our public a harmony of tastes, a "sympathy" in the etymological sense of the word, thanks to which our opinions find a resonance there. It is neither possible nor desirable that these opinions should be accepted as law: it suffices that the critic should have succeeded in establishing enough confidence so that they are taken seriously: adopted, discussed, or refuted, they will have contributed to forming the judgment of the non-specialized reader. They will at least have drawn his attention to a musician or a piece of music which might have escaped him.

To bring some light into these shadowy zones, to help in placing a work in its context, to aid a composer or an interpreter too modest to claim his place in the sun, to reduce to their just proportions the successes of snobbism—these are the tasks whose usefulness seems to me evident and that enter into the sphere of the daily critic. I should be content, for my part, to have honestly acquitted these tasks and to have merited as an epitaph these few words by Faguet on Brunetière: "He performed very well his job as a critic, which consists in stimulating thought."

Since I have protested against an article in which music criticism is ill-used, one might think that I have set myself up as its defender. Nothing is further from my thoughts: one cannot defend what does not exist, and I believe, with many others whose judgment inspires my confidence, that at the moment Music Criticism, with capital letters, does not exist.

To condemn or to praise it on a world-wide scale seems to me to be as senseless as to condemn or to praise Contemporary Composers, when there are in music today almost as many diverse tendencies as there are living composers.

This diversity of tendencies, of minds, of cultures exists no less among the critics, who are united on occasion by practical problems, as is the case in any trade group, but whose unity does not extend beyond such interests. In truth, one does not see how it could be otherwise, given the way in which our recruitment operates: without fixed rules, even without usages firmly enough established to have the force of law. The older I get, the more I am struck by what a motley crowd forms our profession, where the spread of merit, of ability, of background, of sensibility seems to me infinitely greater than in other branches of criticism, primarily because of the extreme fantasy that presides over our recruitment. If any proof is needed, I have not far to look.

I blush retrospectively in recalling my beginning. Nineteen years old, a student, I intended to become a musicologist, although no one suspected. My friends knew that I scraped on the violin and that I was more assiduous in frequenting the peanut galleries of the concert halls than the lecture halls of Professors Lanson, Courbaud, Michaut, and colleagues. One of my friends asked me pointblank one day: "How would you like to write music criticism for such-and-such a review?" I declined, citing my incompetence. Positively scandalized, he replied, "So what? I do *The Doctor's Notebook!*" As he had barely started his second year of medical school, the argument carried weight. It only remained for me to arm myself with an impenetrable pseudonym and to begin, doubly reassured by the incognito and the inner conviction that no one would read me, the journal being obscure and its director almost illiterate. (Parenthetically, I had the surprise of seeing that not only were the heroes and the victims of my articles aware of the distressing sheet, but they took the trouble to send me corrections, recriminations, or thanks: not the very great, not Debussy, or Fauré, or Ravel, but the demi-gods whom I, in a stupor, saw climb down from their pedestals to make friends with the greenhorn that I was.)

One gets used to everything. I soon came to consider myself a critic. But if the idea had come to anyone to group me, in praise or blame, with the authorities of the time, with Laloy, Marnold, Pierre Lalo, Vuillermoz, I think I should have found the notion absolutely comical.

Today, as yesterday, it is a delicate thing to generalize about our profession. It has neither code nor bible. The dogmatic treatises which try to establish one all come up against the irreducible subjectivity of our judgments: we have not even succeeded in defining "the beautiful in music." And I hasten to add that I have no remedy to suggest for the present. The School for Critics, with exercises in the manual of the pen, in discipline, in target practice, under the surveillance of Adjutant Beckmesser, would perhaps furnish the bulk of the troops in a regimented criticism; but not the heads of the line, who cannot be obtained by that sort of drill.

The solution will be longer in coming. When music acquires as much importance in social life as sport, fashion, or the movies, then and only then will the serious press, guided by statistics, grant to music criticism a place in proportion to its presumed interest to the readers. From which it will follow that the profession will be one on which one can live without a second job. Only then can one envisage a professional discipline, not more standardized than in the domains of literature or the drama, but resting on solid and verifiable bases. Only then will more prospective candidates be drawn to the field, whom it will be proper to encourage. Only then can there be a question of a community of doctrine.

Until that happy time, let us accept each music critic for what he is, without saddling him with the responsibility, or a part of the responsibility, for the actions of a collective monster which one would be hard put to it to define.

And if you are absolutely set on a willful attack on this mythical being, do not ask it of a savant of the laboratory.

Entrust it rather to a man of the profession. It is a game that many of them love to play in their idle moments, when there is no one else to devour.

I have been rereading the old columns of the late Ernest Newman, who was for so long the dean of London music critics. To one who did not know that he was one of us and who had no experience with the redoubtable British humor, he would appear to be the sworn enemy of our profession, for no one ridiculed it more often or more cruelly than he did.

Often he did it from the outside, so to speak. For example, he described with the precision of a Fabre observing insects "the avant-garde critic" who fastens on each new movement and uses it as a pedestal to raise himself, who swallows slogans and passwords with the sole desire of being the first champion of such-and-such a composer—as ridiculous in his way and as pathetic as any reactionary Hanslick or Artusi. "He ignores the insidious way history has of taking a different turn from what was expected. He detects what he thinks will be the cat of the future, leaps in the direction the cat has leapt in, without realizing the sad comic figure he will make if, as sometimes happens, the cat beats a retreat, tired, footsore, leaving his too impulsive followers stranded in a critical no man's land . . ."

Sometimes he amuses himself by assuming one of the faults freely imputed to us by artists who think they have not received their just allowance of praise; he plays the fool, the man who can be bought, the hypocrite, the cynic.

He wrote a side-splitting article on a concert given without the names of the composers (analogous to the one given by the Société Internationale de Musique which turned out so badly, in 1911, when Léo Sachs was taken for Schumann and Ravel for a joker!). One finds passages such as this: "These good people, the critics, have enough trials to endure without being asked to decide publicly who is the author of a piece and what its value is. It will be objected that they pass their time making easy pronouncements on such and such a piece of music. Yes, but we have the name of the composer to help us, and that makes all the difference . . . For the moment, a few simple rules serve to guide my practice. I have a vague idea of what ought to be thought about a piece, provided someone has told me if it is a symphony or an opera, if it is by Beethoven, by Bach, by Wagner, or some other well-known person. But to sit through a concert without knowing if one is listening to fugues, symphonies, scherzos, or tangos, and who the devil wrote the confounded things, that is enough to drive any critic crazy. And to find out the next day that one has turned up one's nose at a Bach Passion, taking it for a bit of fluff by Coleridge Taylor, or has praised Brahms for a laborious composition by Ebenezer Prout! . . ."

Another day it is a bravura piece in favor of venality: "I do not think that any critic sees an objection in principle to letting himself be bought—if I dare describe in vulgar language what should be a delicate and charming business. For my part, I don't see any; all that I ask is that the sum be large enough to make it worthwhile. I have my price, like the others, and no intention of lowering it. A whiskey and soda or a cigar offered by a tenor, a wink from a soprano is not enough. Let them offer me what I could get in the football pools—a car, a pension in the neighborhood of 1000 pounds a year, a villa at Brighton, and I shall take it under consideration . . ."

Or else he writes gravely on the necessity of having a bad character: "Since it has been established medically that as other men speak according to their knowledge, the music critic always speaks according to his liver, you must do everything to undermine your liver, methodically, of course, while staying healthy and happy in the intervals between your obligations as a critic . . ."

Elsewhere, some variations on the antipathy the critic should inspire: "After all, the critic is more at ease with hostility than with friendship: the latter is a variable quantity, the former presents a satisfying finality. No man, whose horrible profession it is to criticize others, can foresee how long he can keep a friend; but he knows that an enemy is forever . . . and although the critic cannot hope to attract the friendship of someone merely because he desires it, the number of enemies he can make depends entirely on himself." Lastly I shall mention a four-page column on newspaper obituaries, written with a perfectly assumed cynicism: "Death comes soon or late to every man; but a great man who lives quietly and safely at home, and who can more or less choose the time of his death, has not the right to quit this life without remembering his debts of honor to his journalistic biographers. On this subject I speak with emotion, for several of these gentlemen have put me to great embarrassment by their irregular and inconsiderate manner of dying . . . The death of Goldmark has taken us unawares: we thought he had been dead for years. And it is only recently that I discovered that Max Bruch is still living, an octogenarian. Now that I have concocted a careful obituary, he will probably live to be a hundred . . ."

Granted that these tirades—and I have shortened them

ridiculously—make the article against which I protested seem very pale. But observe also that Ernest Newman articulates only one grievance at a time—one to a column. It makes me think of a story by Pierre Mille, in which we see Nasr-ed-Din, a worthy Mussulman, looking over the slave market in search of a wife. The merchant shows him one with a pretty face, but she limps; another with a lovely body, but she squints; with a third, it is the voice that is disagreeable. And as Nasr-ed-Din complains of these imperfections, the merchant replies calmly: "If you want several qualities, take several wives!"

Likewise, you who criticize the critics, if you wish to destroy them, do not impute every fault to every critic. Such a complete harmony, even in evil, is not probable. It has something inhuman, or superhuman, which becomes almost flattering, and which, consequently, it is good policy to avoid.